CHRISTIAN LIFE FAITH
AND THOUGHT

CHRISTIAN LIFE
FAITH AND THOUGHT
IN THE
SOCIETY OF FRIENDS

*Being the First Part of
the Christian Discipline
of the Religious Society of
Friends in Great Britain*

*Approved and adopted by Yearly Meeting
1921*

*Published by the Central Offices of
the Religious Society of Friends*

and obtainable from

Friends Book Centre
Friends House, Euston Road, London, N.W.1

This Edition first printed 1922
Reprinted 1922, 1923, 1927
Reprinted in present form, 1942, 1943 *and* 1945
Reprinted, with slight revision, 1950

PRINTED IN GREAT BRITAIN BY HEADLEY BROTHERS
109 KINGSWAY, LONDON, W.C.2; AND ASHFORD, KENT

CONTENTS

CHAPTER   PAGE

PREFACE - - - - - - - - vi

INTRODUCTORY - - - - - - - 1

I SPIRITUAL EXPERIENCES OF FRIENDS - - 5

II CONCERNING CREEDS - - - - - 64

III GENERAL DOCTRINAL STATEMENTS - - - 66

IV THE LIGHT OF CHRIST IN THE HEART - - 71

V THE NATURE OF GOD AND HIS UNIVERSAL GRACE 82

VI THE PERSON AND WORK OF JESUS CHRIST - 86

VII THE SCRIPTURES - - - - - - 98

VIII THE CHURCH - - - - - - - 103

IX THE WAY OF LIFE - - - - - - 108

X RELIGIOUS PROBLEMS - - - - - 131

PRAYER FROM *Essays and Addresses* BY JOHN
WILHELM ROWNTREE, AND EXTRACT FROM
JOHN WOOLMAN *Journal* - - - - 139

INDEX OF PERSONS AND AUTHORITIES (including
Scripture references) - - - - - 140

INDEX OF SUBJECTS - - - - - - 144

PREFACE

Extracts from the Minutes and Advices of the Yearly Meeting of Friends held in London was published by it in 1783 and 1802. A third and enlarged edition in 1834 included for the first time extracts from the epistle written by George Fox and others in 1671 to the Governor of Barbados, and other extracts relating to Christian doctrine. Fourth and fifth editions were issued by the Yearly Meetings of 1861 and 1883, the book being divided into three sections, *Christian Doctrine*, *Christian Practice*, *Christian Discipline*. The section on *Christian Practice* was carefully revised in the four years preceding 1911, and was issued as a separate volume by the Yearly Meeting in that year.* The section on *Christian Discipline* entitled *Church Government* was also issued separately, and is kept up to date by including in the new copies issued any fresh regulations made by the Yearly Meeting.†

In 1919 the Yearly Meeting directed the holding of a representative conference to consider the question of revising the section on Christian Doctrine, with power to bring forward a draft revision. In 1920 the first draft of the present volume was prepared and early in 1921 was carefully revised by the conference for submission to the Yearly Meeting, which approved it, subject to final revision by an editorial committee.

The book, besides many paragraphs from the edition of the section on Christian Doctrine, issued in 1883, includes so much additional material from the writings of deceased Friends and from Society documents that it is substantially a new work. The title, " Christian Life, Faith and Thought in the Society of Friends ", shows the character now given to the book. The attempt has been made throughout to state truth, not by formulating it, but by expressing it through the vital personal and

* A thoroughly revised and largely re-written edition of *Christian Practice* was approved by the Yearly Meeting and published in 1925.

† The last complete revision was approved in 1931.

corporate experience of Friends. Life itself, with its variety of outlook and condition, seems to us the way by which God has spoken to men through the prophets, and supremely through Jesus Christ, and by which His living Spirit has spoken and is still speaking to men.

The opening section of the book, entitled " Spiritual Experiences of Friends," has been compiled with this object, not as a record of Friends of the past, but as a limited selection of a few vital experiences sufficient to illustrate the varied ways in which the heavenly vision has come with living power to the souls of men. The Yearly Meeting approved the addition of brief biographical and explanatory notes, and for these the editorial committee is solely responsible.

In the other sections, careful attention should be paid to the dates of the different documents and extracts. These we believe were all vital expressions of truth as it was understood at the time they were written, but modes of thought and utterance change, and, while the central truths remain, their statement, if re-written by the Society to-day, would no doubt vary on subordinate points. The subjects of Christian thought and life are inseparable, and as the present volume may have a large circulation apart from the volume on Christian Practice, it has been thought essential to include a section on " The Way of Life." This contains a selection of extracts which might well find a place in any future edition of the volume on Christian Practice, and that volume should be consulted for a fuller treatment of many of the subjects.

It is hoped that the book, with its emphasis throughout on vital experience, may prove an inspiration not only to our own members, but to many in other sections of the Church universal and to seekers after truth everywhere.

The harvest from which we have gathered is a rich one and will be added to continually in future years. We do not regard the collection we have made as in any sense a final expression of the truth of God or of religious experience. We look forward to additions and alterations being made from time to time and would welcome them with joy and gladness. We shall be satisfied if this edition can be described in the words of the inspiring extract narrating the voyage of the *Woodhouse*: "We went forth and gathered sticks, and kindled a fire and left it burning."

Dearly beloved Friends, these things we do not lay upon you as a rule or form to walk by, but that all, with the measure of light which is pure and holy, may be guided : and so in the light walking and abiding, these may be fulfilled in the Spirit, not in the letter, for the letter killeth, but the Spirit giveth life.— (Postscript to the Letter from the Meeting of Elders at Balby, near Doncaster, 1656, the earliest advice on Christian practice issued by any general body of Friends. *Letters of Early Friends*, p. 282.)

All truth is a shadow except the last—except the utmost, yet every truth is true in its kind. It is substance in its own place, though it be but a shadow in another place (for it is but a shadow from an intenser substance) ; and the shadow is a true shadow, as the substance is a true substance.—Isaac Penington (1616-1679), quoted by Elizabeth Waterhouse. *A Little Book of Life and Death*, p. 145.

It is not opinion, or speculation, or notions of what is true, or assent to or the subscription of articles or propositions, though never so soundly worded, that . . . makes a man a true believer or a true Christian. But it is a conformity of mind and practice to the will of God, in all holiness of conversation, according to the dictates of this Divine principle of Light and Life in the soul which denotes a person truly a child of God. —William Penn (1644-1718). *A Key*, published in 1692, from *Works*, 1726 edition, vol. II, p. 781.

INTRODUCTORY .

Reality in Religion

These are no days for anything that is not vital. If there is one word that expresses the demand of men in regard to religion, it is reality. Creeds that cannot be translated into life and conduct do not touch us. . . . We need to experience for ourselves the imposition of the piercèd hands, so that, amid the voices of the modern world, and in the pressure of modern business, we may know as our own the experience of the Apostle :—
" For the love of Christ constraineth us ; because we thus judge, that one died for all, therefore all died ; and He died for all, that they which live should no longer live unto themselves, but unto Him who for their sakes died and rose again." This constraining love is the strength of the Christian's life. Our Lord's appeal to us is based not on a scheme of ethics, not on a creed, but on devotion to Himself. " If ye love Me, ye will keep My commandments." . . . The world still demands, in the greatness of its need, a real Saviour ; for its sin can nowhere else find forgiveness than at His cross, and its sorrows can nowhere else find solace than in His love.

Yet of those who, entering the Kingdom, find in their Lord new life for their own souls, how few there are who fully understand that the great law of that Kingdom is a law of service for others. In other words, they have failed to see the two-fold aspect of our Lord's redemptive work, which has power to transform, not only the individual, but also society as a whole.

We are saved that we may serve, and the church that grasps this wide conception of the law of service, and acts upon it, is the church of the coming day. . . . Quakerism should not be the cult of a few, but the life of a multitude. In the first instance it owed its vitality to the fact that it brought back to professing Christians the living power of the first message of

Christ. "Union with Christ" was its inherent and persistent theme. We believe :—

"There is room yet for a fellowship, all-inclusive in its tender sympathy ; drawn close in the loving bondage of sincerity and truth ; for a noble simplicity of life and manners, rich in true culture and the taste born of knowledge ; for a freedom that scorns the flummeries of rank, the perquisites of pride, because it knows the worth of manhood and loves the privilege of friendship ; for a simple worship, homely and informal because intimate and real.

"Climb Pendle Hill with Fox, and see once more his vision, ' a great people to be gathered ' ; enter in spirit the dungeons of the past and learn why they were palaces, and the bolts precious jewels ; repeat again with Nayler his tender words, and, in the spirit of his message face the future that lies before you : ' There is a spirit that delights to do no evil, nor to revenge any wrong . . . its crown is meekness, its life is everlasting love unfeigned, it takes its kingdom with entreaty and not with contention, and keeps it by lowliness of mind.' "*—From the *Yearly Meeting Epistle*, 1905.

Faith and Belief

In regard to the use of the word " faith " for the body of beliefs which a Christian Church holds, the Society of Friends has never been content to use the word with a purely intellectual connotation. The faith which is essential to Christianity it conceives to be a much deeper thing—the response of a man's whole being to the love and grace of God when this is inwardly revealed to him. It is not only a belief in truth (cognitive), but a surrender to truth (volitional). In George Fox's words it is " that which purifieth the heart, which gives the victory . . . over that which separates from God ; in which faith was the unity of the saints in the primitive times, in which also stands our unity." (*Some Principles of the elect People of God, in scorn called Quakers*, sec. vii., 1661.) To think that we have defined

* John Wilhelm Rowntree, *Essays and Addresses*, 1906, pp. 75, 76.

our faith when we have only defined the cognitive side of it, is to treat the definition of the less important part of it as if it were the definition of the whole. If this definition is imposed as an article of faith, we shall only secure a Christianity of notions instead of a Christianity of experience. . . .

We conceive of Christianity not as a collection of " notions " or doctrines, and a number of traditional observances ; but as essentially an experience, and a way of life based on that experience. Christian unity for us consists not in agreement in ideas and practices, but in a common *Christian experience*, apart from which neither doctrines nor practices appear to us to have meaning or value. The doctrines of Christianity are in our judgment intended to interpret the fundamental facts of Christian experience—the objective facts of the person and work of Jesus Christ, handed down to us by some of those who knew them at first hand ; and the subjective facts (both individual and collective) of redemption from sin and communion with God through Him. And the practices of our religion have value only in so far as they maintain and develop this inward experience and the life that flows from it. . . . To us [the unity of Christians] consists in the one divine life that is reproducing in them the character of the historic person, Jesus Christ ; which, while it is something far deeper than any definition of His person, is for Christians the final manifestation of the character of God Himself. " The glory which Thou has given Me I have given them, that they all may be one."

That, we believe, has always been the Quaker position. The main purpose of the writings of the early Friends, in so far as they were controversial, was to bring back the church from a Christianity of ideas and practices to a Christianity of living experience and conformity to the mind and will of God, which they believed to have been its essential character in the first century. They also insisted that the possibility of this experience was open to every human soul, and not only to a privileged few ; that there was no exclusive priesthood, and no prescribed ceremony through which alone it could be received. . . . The experience in which these Quaker writers found the true basis of unity was something much more than a religion of feeling or passing emotion. It arose from a common love and loyalty to Him whose love had won their hearts, and expressed itself in a definite type of Christian character and conduct, in a life of inward holiness and practical service to men. . . .

It is not in the life itself, but in the attempt to formulate its implications, and to fix it by uniform religious practices, that divisions arise. We do not in the least deprecate the attempt, which must be made, since man is a rational being, to formulate intellectually the ideas which are implicit in religious experience. . . . But it should always be recognised that all such attempts are provisional, and can never be assumed to possess the finality of ultimate truth. There must always be room for development and progress, and Christian thought and inquiry should never be fettered by theory. . . .

Among the dangers of formulated statements of belief are these :—

(1) They tend to crystallise thought on matters that will always be beyond any final embodiment in human language ;

(2) They fetter the search for truth and for its more adequate expression ; and

(3) They set up a fence which tends to keep out of the Christian fold many sincere and seeking souls who would gladly enter it.

Particularly in these days we need to be on our guard against these dangers. Multitudes of people are being shaken out of their comfortable beliefs by the terrific experiences through which the world is passing, and are seeking for a secure basis for their faith. And some are finding a reality which is much too great to be confined within the narrow limits of a creed. —From a *Statement on The True Basis of Christian Unity*, presented to the Yearly Meeting, 1917, by its Commission appointed in connection with The World Conference on Faith and Order.

CHAPTER I

SPIRITUAL EXPERIENCES OF FRIENDS

George Fox (1624-1691), the Founder of the Quaker Movement, was the son of a Leicestershire weaver, and was apprenticed to a shoemaker and wooldealer. His *Journal*, first published in 1694 after his death, ranks among the great religious autobiographies of the world. The early extracts that follow show how he reached his own first-hand experience of Christ, after wide acquaintance with Puritanism in all its forms. Sentences which have been added from William Penn and Thomas Ellwood (the editor of the *Journal*), show the vivid impression made by his personality. The draft *Journal* 1649-1675 is extant, and has been published in two volumes by the Cambridge University Press, 1911, edited with full notes by Norman Penney.

As I had forsaken all the priests, so I left the separate preachers also, and those called the most-experienced people. For I saw there was none among them all that could speak to my condition. And when all my hopes in them and in all men was gone, so that I had nothing outwardly to help me, nor could tell what to do, then, O then, I heard a voice which said, " There is one, even Christ Jesus, that can speak to thy condition," and, when I heard it, my heart did leap for joy. Then the Lord did let me see why there was none upon the earth that could speak to my condition, namely, that I might give Him all the glory. For all are concluded under sin and shut up in unbelief, as I had been, that Jesus Christ might have the pre-eminence, who enlightens and gives grace and faith and power. Thus, when God doth work, who shall let it ? And this I knew experimentally. My desires after the Lord grew stronger, and zeal in the pure knowledge of God and of Christ alone, without the help of any man, book or writing. For though I read the Scriptures that spake of Christ and of God, yet I knew Him not, but by revelation, as He who hath the key did open, and as the Father of Life drew me to His Son by His Spirit. And then the Lord did gently lead me along, and did let me see His love, which was endless and eternal, and surpasseth all the knowledge that men have in the natural state or can get by history or books : and that love did let me see myself as I was without Him. . . . And when I myself was in the deep, under all shut up, I could not believe that I should ever overcome : my troubles, my sorrows and my temptations were so great that I thought many times I should have despaired, I was so tempted. But when Christ opened to me how He was tempted by the same devil, and had overcome him and bruised his head, and that through Him and His power, light, grace and Spirit I should overcome also, I had confidence in Him. So He it was that opened to me, when I was shut up and had not hope nor faith. Christ it was, who had enlightened me, that gave me His light to believe in, and gave me hope, which is Himself, revealed Himself in me, and gave me His Spirit, and gave me His grace which I found sufficient in the deeps and in weakness. Thus, in the deepest miseries, and in the greatest sorrows and temptations that many times beset me, the Lord in His mercy did keep me. And I found that there were two thirsts in me the one after the creatures to have gotten help and strength there, and the other after the Lord, the Creator, and His Son, Jesus Christ. And I saw all the world could do me no good ; if I had had a king's diet, palace and attendance, all would have been as nothing ; for nothing gave me comfort but the Lord by His power.—*Journal*, 1694 edition, pp. 8, 9. Bi-centenary edition, 1891, vol. I, pp. 11-13.

1647 : I was under great temptations sometimes, and my inward sufferings were heavy ; but I could find none to open my condition to, but the Lord alone, unto whom I cried night and day. And I went back into Nottinghamshire, and there the Lord shewed me that the natures of those things, which were hurtful without, were within in the hearts and minds of wicked men. The natures of dogs, swine, vipers, of Sodom and Egypt, Pharaoh, Cain, Ishmael, Esau, etc., the natures of these I saw within, though people had been looking without. And I cried to the Lord, saying, " Why should I be thus, seeing I was never addicted to commit those evils ? " And the Lord answered, That it was needful I should have a sense of all conditions : how else should I speak to all conditions ? And in this I saw the infinite love of God. I saw also that there was an ocean of darkness and death, but an infinite ocean of light and love, which flowed over the ocean of darkness : and in that also I saw the infinite love of God ; and I had great openings.

And, as I was walking by the steeple-house side in the town of Mansfield, the Lord said unto me, " That which people do trample upon must be thy food." And, as the Lord spake, He opened it to me how that people and professors did trample upon the Life, even the Life of Christ was trampled upon : and they fed upon words : and fed one another with words, but trampled upon the Life, and trampled under foot the blood of the Son of God (which blood was my Life) and they lived in their airy notions, talking of Him. It seemed strange to me at the first that I should feed on that which the high professors trampled upon ; but the Lord opened it clearly to me by His eternal Spirit and power.—*Journal*, 1694 edition, p. 13. Bi-centenary edition, 1891, vol. I, pp. 19, 20.

1645 : Priest Stevens asked me a question—*viz.*, why Christ cried out upon the cross, " My God, my God, why hast thou forsaken me ? " and why He said, " If it be possible, let this cup pass from me ; yet not my will but thine be done " ? And I told him, " At that time the sins of all mankind were upon Him, and their iniquities and transgressions, with which He was wounded ; which He was to bear, and to be an offering for them, as He was man, but died not as He was God. And so in that He died for all men, and tasted death for every man, He was an offering for the sins of the whole world." This I spake, being at that time in a measure sensible of Christ's sufferings and what He went through.—*Journal*, 1694 edition, p. 4. Bi-centenary edition, 1891, vol. I, p. 5.

In his testimony or ministry he much laboured to open truth to people's understandings, and to bottom them upon the principle and principal, Christ Jesus the Light of the World, that by bringing them to something that was of God in themselves, they might the better know and judge of Him and themselves.

He had an extraordinary gift in opening the Scriptures. He would go to the marrow of things, and show the mind, harmony and fulfilling of them with much plainness and to great comfort and edification.

But above all he excelled in prayer. The inwardness and weight of his spirit, the reverence and solemnity of his address and behaviour, and the fewness and fullness of his words have often struck even strangers with admiration, as they used to reach others with consolation. The most awful, living, reverent frame I ever felt or beheld, I must say, was his in prayer. And truly it was a testimony he knew and lived nearer to the Lord than other men ; for they that know Him most will see most reason to approach Him with reverence and fear.—William Penn's Preface to Fox's *Journal*, Bi-centenary edition, 1891, vol. I, p. xlviii.

He was indeed an heavenly-minded man, zealous for the name of the Lord, and preferred the honour of God before all things. He was valiant for the truth, bold in asserting it, patient in suffering for it, unwearied in labouring in it, steady in his testimony to it, immovable as a rock.—Thomas Ellwood's Testimony to George Fox, *Journal*, 1694 edition, p. xvi., Bi-centenary edition, 1891, vol. II, p. 526.

Divers Friends came to visit him in his illness, unto some of whom he said : " All is well ; the Seed of God reigns over all and over death itself."—His dying words, *Journal*, 1694 edition, pp. 613, 614. Bi-centenary edition, 1891, vol. II, p. 506.

The Early Friends. Experiences recorded by William Penn (1644-1718).

As [the Word of Light and Life] reached the conscience and broke the heart, and brought many to a sense and search, so what people had been vainly seeking *without* with much pains and cost, they by this ministry found *within*, where it was they wanted what they sought for, *viz.* : the right way to peace with God. For they were directed to the Light of Jesus Christ within them, as the seed and leaven of the Kingdom of God, near all because *in* all and God's talent to all, a faithful and true witness and just monitor *in* every bosom, the gift and grace of God to life and salvation that appears to all though few

regard it. This, the traditional Christian, conceited of himself and strong in his own will and righteousness and overcome with blind zeal and passion, either despised as a low and common thing or opposed as a novelty under many hard names or opprobrious terms, denying in his ignorant and angry mind any fresh manifestation of God's power and Spirit in man in these days, though never more needed to make true Christians ; not unlike those Jews of old, that rejected the Son of God at the very same time that they blindly professed to wait for the Messiah to come, because, alas, He appeared not among them according to their carnal mind and expectation. . . . .
—William Penn's Preface to Fox's *Journal*, Bi-centenary edition, 1891, vol. I, p. xxvi.

They were changed men themselves before they went about to change others. Their hearts were rent as well as their garments, and they knew the power and work of God upon them. . . . And as they freely received what they had to say from the Lord, so they freely administered it to others. The bent and stress of their ministry was conversion to God, regeneration and holiness, not schemes of doctrines and verbal creeds or new forms of worship, but a leaving off in religion the superfluous and reducing the ceremonious and formal part, and pressing earnestly the substantial, the necessary and profitable part, as all upon a serious reflection must and do acknowledge.
—*Ibid.*, vol. I, p. xxxvii.

William Dewsbury (1621-1688), who came from Allerthorpe in the East Riding of Yorkshire, was one of the sweetest and wisest of the early Quakers. He spent a great part of his life in prison, chiefly at Warwick. His undaunted faith and reconciling spirit contributed greatly to the Quaker movement. The extract given as to his experience in prison may be matched by another in a letter to Bristol Friends, April, 1678 : " When Sion's enemies puts (the Lord's servants) in holes and dungeons, God makes a prison more comfortable than a pleasant palace and fetters of iron far surpassing chains of gold ; yea, He causeth them to sing in tribulation as Paul and Silas did in the stocks." Isaac Penington and others write in the same strain.

I was conceived in sin and brought forth in iniquity, and in that state lived until I was about eight years of age, when the

Word of the Lord came unto me, " I created thee for my glory, an account thou must give to Me for all thy words and actions done in the body," which word enlightened my heart and opened the book of conscience in me.   Then I ceased from my vain conversation, and began to read the Scriptures and books, and mourn and pray to a God I knew not where He was.   They said He was above the skies, calling it Heaven, but I felt the hand of the Lord within me, executing judgment upon the wicked in me, and what way ever I turned to seek Him in observations, thither the flaming sword turned, to keep the way of the tree [of] life and execute the righteous justice of God upon me.

Then it pleased the Lord to order my friends to put me to mind the sheep, where I was retired from company, so my mind was kept in my mournful estate, where my greatest ease was in mourning to a God I knew not.   When I was thirteen years old, I was bound an apprentice to a clothmaker in Holbeck, near Leeds, but I could find no peace in that worship of God the world hath set up, as in receiving the bread and wine, which they told me was the seals of the covenant.   Then much fear seized upon my soul, and Judas' condition was cast into my mind, until it were shewed that the seal of the covenant was the Spirit of Christ and no outward element, and the Supper was the body and blood of Christ, which the world doth not know, nor I at that time.   Then I durst join no more in their practice in singing David's conditions, which they called Psalms, for the light in my conscience let me see the evil of my heart, that I was not in David's condition.   At that time did the wars begin in this nation, and the men called ministers cried, " Curse ye Meroz, because they went not forth to help the Lord against the mighty." Then I was willing to give my body to death, in obedience to my God, to free my soul from sin, and I joined with that little remnant which said they fought for the gospel, but I found no rest to my soul amongst them.   And the word of the Lord came unto me and said, " Put up thy sword into thy scabbard ; if my kingdom were of this world, then would my children fight," which word enlightened my heart and discovered the mystery of iniquity, and that the Kingdom of Christ was within, and the enemies was within, and was spiritual, and my weapons against them must be spiritual, the power of God.

Then I could no longer fight with a carnal weapon against a carnal man, and returned to my outward calling, and my will was brought in subjection for the Lord to do with me what His will was—if He condemned me, He might : and, if He saved me, it was His free love—and in this condemned estate I lay crying in the depth of misery. And the cry of my condemned soul was great, and could not be satisfied, but breathed and thirsted after Christ, to save me freely through His blood or I perished for ever, and in this condemned estate I lay waiting for the coming of Christ Jesus, who, in the appointed time of the Father, appeared to my soul, as the lightnings from the east to the west. And my dead soul heard His voice, and by His voice was made to live, who created me to a lively hope, and sealed me up in the everlasting covenant of life with His blood. Then I witnessed the wages of sin and death, and the gift of God eternal life, through Jesus Christ my Lord.

So through the righteous law of life in Christ Jesus, I was made free and am from the body of sin and death, and through these great tribulations my garments is washed and made white in the blood of the Lamb, who hath led me through the gates of the city into the new Jerusalem, where my soul now feeds upon the Tree of Life, which I had so long hungered and thirsted after, that stands in the paradise of God, where there is no more curse nor night, but the Lord God and the Lamb is my Light and Life for ever and ever. I witness I am regenerated and born again of the immortal Seed.—Abridged from *The Discovery of the Great Enmity of the Serpent* 1655, printed in Dewsbury's *Works*, 1689, pp. 44-54.

For this I can say, I never since played the coward, but joyfully entered prisons as palaces, telling mine enemies to hold me there as long as they could : and in the prison-house I sung praises to my God, and esteemed the bolts and locks put upon me as jewels, and in the Name of the eternal God I alway got the victory, for they could keep me no longer than the determined time of my God.—Dewsbury's *Works*, 1689, early unnumbered page.

If any one has received any good or benefit through this vessel, called William Dewsbury, give God the glory; I'll have none, I'll have none, I'll have none.—*First Publishers of Truth*, 1907, p. 199.

Margaret Fell (1614-1702), afterwards wife of George Fox, was the wife of Judge Thomas Fell, of Swarthmore Hall, near Ulverston, when Fox came there in June, 1652, after his wonderful weeks among the Westmorland Seekers.   Swarthmore Hall became the centre for the Quaker " Publishers of Truth " and Margaret Fell the nursing-mother of the new movement. In 1669, eleven years after her first husband's death, she married Fox, though his service for the Church prevented them from living much together at Swarthmore.   The six Fell daughters who were living at the time of the second marriage all became prominent Friends.

It is interesting to note that three of the servants of the household, mentioned in the extract as convinced by Fox, also became well-known Quaker leaders.   William Caton (1636-1665) was at the time companion to young George Fell, and was one of the apostles of Quakerism in Holland. Thomas Salthouse (1630-1691) laboured chiefly in the south-west of England. Anne Clayton travelled to Barbados and America.   Richard Farnsworth, of Tickhill, Yorkshire, who is also mentioned, had like Dewsbury reached the Quaker experience before he came to know Fox in 1651, and was for several years the chief Quaker leader in Yorkshire and the North Midlands.   He died in 1666.

In the year 1652 it pleased the Lord to draw him [George Fox] towards us. . . . My then husband, Thomas Fell, was not at home at that time, but gone the Welsh circuit, being one of the Judges of Assize, and our house [Swarthmore Hall] being a place open to entertain ministers and religious people at, one of George Fox his friends brought him hither, where he stayed all night.   And the next day, being a lecture or a fast-day, he went to Ulverston steeplehouse, but came not in till people were gathered ; I and my children had been a long time there before.   And when they were singing before the sermon, he came in ; and when they had done singing, he stood up upon a seat or form and desired that he might have liberty to speak. And he that was in the pulpit said he might.   And the first words that he spoke were as followeth : " He is not a Jew that is one outward, neither is that circumcision which is outward ; but he is a Jew that is one inward, and that is circumcision which is of the heart." And so he went on and said, How that Christ was the Light of the world and lighteth every man that cometh into the world ; and that by this Light they might be gathered to God, &c. And I stood up in my pew, and I wondered at his doctrine, for I had never heard such before. And then he went on, and opened the Scriptures, and said, " The Scriptures were the prophets' words and Christ's and the apostles' words, and what as they spoke they enjoyed and possessed and had it from the Lord." And said, " Then what had any to do with the Scriptures, but as they came to the Spirit that gave them forth. You will say, Christ saith this, and the apostles say this ; but what canst thou say ? Art thou a child of Light and hast walked in the Light, and what thou speakest is it inwardly from God ? &c."

This opened me so that it cut me to the heart ; and then I saw clearly we were all wrong. So I sat me down in my pew again, and cried bitterly. And I cried in my spirit to the Lord, " We are all thieves, we are all thieves, we have taken the Scriptures in words and know nothing of them in ourselves." So that served me, that I cannot well tell what he spake afterwards ; but he went on in declaring against the false prophets and priests and deceivers of the people.

And there was one John Sawrey, a Justice of Peace and a professor, that bid the churchwarden " Take him away," and he laid his hands on him several times, and took them off again and let him alone ; and then after a while he gave over and came to our house again that night. And he spoke in the family amongst the servants ; and they were all generally convinced, as William Caton, Thomas Salthouse, Mary Askew, Anne Clayton and several other servants. And I was stricken into such a sadness I knew not what to do, my husband being from home. I saw it was the truth, and I could not deny it ; and I did, as the apostle saith, I " received the truth in the love of it." And it was opened to me so clear that I had never a tittle in my heart against it ; but I desired the Lord that I might be kept in it, and then I desired no greater portion.

And then he went on . . . and abundance were convinced and saw that which he spoke was truth, but the priests were all in a rage. And about two weeks after, James Nayler and Richard Farnsworth followed him, and inquired him out till they came to Swarthmore, and there stayed awhile with me at our house and did me much good ; for I was under great heaviness and judgment. But the power of the Lord entered upon me within about two weeks that he came ; and about three weeks' end my husband came home. . . . And any may think what a condition I was like to be in, that either I might displease my husband or offend God ; for he was very much troubled with us all in the house and family, [the neighbours] had so prepossessed him against us. But James Nayler and Richard Farnsworth were both then at our house. . . . And after that he had heard them speak awhile, he was better satisfied ; and they offered as if they would go away ; but I desired them to stay, and not to go away yet, for George Fox will come this evening. . . . And then was he pretty moderate and quiet, and his dinner being ready he went to it, and I went in and sat me down by him. And whilst I was sitting, the power of the Lord seized upon me ; and he was stricken with amazement, and knew not what to think, but was quiet and still. And the children were all quiet and still and grown sober, and could not play on their music that they were learning, and all these things made him quiet and still.

And then at night George Fox came . . . and he spoke very excellently as ever I heard him. . . . And so my husband came to see clearly the truth of what he spoke, and was very quiet that night, and said no more and went to bed. And next morning . . . at our house, divers Friends were speaking one to another . . . where to get a meeting. My husband . . . overheard and said of his own accord, " You may meet here if you will." . . . And there was a good large meeting the First-day, which was the first meeting that was at Swarthmore, and so continued there a meeting from 1652 till 1690.—Margaret

Fox's Testimony to George Fox, *Journal*, 1694 edition, p. ii. Bi-centenary edition, 1891, vol. II, pp. 512-514.

The Swarthmore Household. This impression of the Swarthmore household, in 1653, was written by Anthony Pearson (*c.* 1628-1665), of Rampshaw Hall, Durham, who was a Justice in three counties, and had been Secretary to the Parliamentary leader, Sir Arthur Hesilrige. He was convinced on the Bench in 1653 by hearing James Nayler's spiritual experience. For several years he took a leading part in shaping Quakerism in the North of England, but fell away from Friends about 1659. His eager anti-royalist activities in this year compromised him after the Restoration, but he succeeded in making terms with the authorities.

All my religion was but the hearing of the ear, the believing and talking of a God and Christ in heaven or a place at a distance, I knew not where.

Oh, how gracious was the Lord to me in carrying me to Judge Fell's, to see the wonders of His power and wisdom, a family walking in the fear of the Lord, conversing daily with Him, crucified to the world and living only to God. I was so confounded, all my knowledge and wisdom became folly ; my mouth was stopped, my conscience convinced and the secrets of my heart were made manifest, and that Lord was discovered to be near, whom I ignorantly worshipped.—*Letters of Early Friends*, 1841, p. 11.

James Nayler (1616-1660). James Nayler uttered these words about two hours before his death. The gloom of Nayler's hour of darkness and the glory of his recovery, which make one of the most dramatic chapters in Quaker history, can only be slightly sketched here. He came from the neighbourhood of Wakefield, and in 1653 his moving recital of his own spiritual experience, when he came before the Westmorland Justices on a charge of blasphemy, brought about the convincement to Quakerism of Anthony Pearson. In 1655, Nayler came south to help in work in London, where he became ensnared by flatterers, who behaved themselves in an extravagant fashion, bowing, kneeling and singing before him. On going to Bristol he was persuaded by Friends there to see Fox, then in Launceston jail, but on the way was taken and imprisoned at Exeter. He was freed in October, 1656, and a few days later entered Bristol on horseback with his followers round him. They spread garments before him and sang, " Holy, Holy, Holy, Lord God of Israel." The authorities interfered and sent him to London, where Parliament after long debates sentenced him to imprisonment after being whipped and pilloried in London and Bristol, and branded for a blasphemer, and having his tongue bored through.

Nayler, physically and mentally overstrained, had allowed his flatterers to treat him, in an extravagant fashion, as a Sign to the Nation that Christ was come. He bore his punishments with meekness and soon came to see and publicly to condemn his error. After his release in 1659, he lived in "great self-denial and was very jealous of himself." His Quaker service was resumed in London, and a year later he set out on foot for the North, intending to go home to his wife and children at Wakefield. He was seen by a Friend of Hertford, sitting by the wayside in meditation, and passed on through Huntingdon, where another Friend saw him "in such an awful frame (of mind) as if he had been redeemed from the earth and a stranger on it, seeking a better country and inheritance." Some miles beyond Huntingdon he was robbed and bound, and found towards evening in a field. He was taken to a Friend's house near King's Ripton, and passed away in the peace of God towards the end of October, 1660. The following extract gives his last words, which are perhaps the most beautiful expression in the language of the spirit that has passed beyond martyrdom into peace.

There is a spirit which I feel that delights to do no evil, nor to revenge any wrong, but delights to endure all things, in hope to enjoy its own in the end. Its hope is to outlive all wrath and contention, and to weary out all exaltation and cruelty, or whatever is of a nature contrary to itself. It sees to the end of all temptations. As it bears no evil in itself, so it conceives none in thoughts to any other. If it be betrayed, it bears it, for its ground and spring is the mercies and forgiveness of God. Its crown is meekness, its life is everlasting love unfeigned; it takes its kingdom with entreaty and not with contention, and keeps it by lowliness of mind. In God alone it can rejoice, though none else regard it, or can own its life. It's conceived in sorrow, and brought forth without any to pity it, nor doth it murmur at grief and oppression. It never rejoiceth but through sufferings : for with the world's joy it is murdered. I found it alone, being forsaken. I have fellowship therein with them who lived in dens and desolate places in the earth, who through death obtained this resurrection and eternal holy life.

Thou wast with me when I fled from the face of mine enemies : then didst Thou warn me in the night : Thou carriedst me in Thy power into the hiding-place Thou hadst prepared for me ; there Thou coveredst me with Thy Hand, that in time Thou mightst bring me forth a rock before all the world. When I was weak Thou stayedst me with Thy Hand, that in Thy time Thou mightst present me to the world in Thy strength in which I stand, and cannot be moved. Praise the Lord, O my soul. Let this be written for those that come after. Praise the Lord. J.N.—*Works*, 1716, p. 696 ; the concluding sentences " Thou wast with me," etc., as quoted in Robert Rich, *Hidden Things brought to Light*, 1678, pp. 21, 22.

The Westmorland Seekers (1652). Recent historical research has shown that the existence of a strong Seeker community in Westmorland in 1652, with its centre at Preston Patrick, prepared the way for the success which attended the work of Fox. A large part of this community joined the new movement, which at once became furnished with a band of ardent young men and women who could carry the message to the rest of England. The glowing experience which came to them with the visit of Fox is expressed by Francis Howgill (1618-1669) in the following passage. He came from Todthorne, near Grayrigg, Westmorland, had been a preacher among the Seekers, and was among the foremost workers in London, Bristol, Ireland and elsewhere. For passages from his writings, see p. 72. He died in the prison on Appleby Bridge in January, 1669. His bosom friend, Edward Burrough (1633-1663), from Underbarrow, shared his service, and is called on the title-page of his works, " a son of thunder and consolation, that true prophet and faithful servant of God, and sufferer for the testimony of Jesus, who died a prisoner for the Word of God in the City of London." " His very strength," says Howgill, " was bended after God." And Fox spoke of him as one " who never turned his back on the Truth nor his back from any out of the Truth."

There was more sincerity and true love amongst us and desires after the living, powerful presence of God than was among many in that day who ran into heaps and forms but left the cross behind them. When we had turned aside from hireling shepherds' tents, we found Him whom our souls loved ; and God, out of His great love and great mercy, sent one unto us, a man of God [George Fox], one of ten thousand, to instruct us in the way of God more perfectly. His testimony reached unto all our consciences and entered into the inmost part of our hearts, which drove us to a narrow search and to a diligent inquisition concerning our state, through the Light of Christ Jesus. The Lord of heaven and earth we found to be near at hand, and, as we waited upon Him in pure silence, our minds out of all things, His heavenly presence appeared in our assemblies, when there was no language, tongue nor speech from any creature. The Kingdom of heaven did gather us and catch us all, as in a net, and His heavenly power at one time drew many hundreds to land. We came to know a place to stand in and what to wait in ; and the Lord appeared daily to us, to our astonishment, amazement and great admiration, insomuch that we often said one unto another, with great joy of heart : " What, is the Kingdom of God come to be with men ? And will He take up His tabernacle among the sons of men, as He did of old ? And what ? Shall we, that were reckoned as the outcasts of Israel, have this honour of glory communicated amongst us, which were but men of small parts and of little abilities, in respect of many others, as amongst men ? "

And from that day forward, our hearts were knit unto the Lord and one unto another in true and fervent love, in the covenant of Life with God ; and that was as a strong bond upon all our spirits, which united us one unto another. We met together in the unity of the Spirit, and of the bond of peace, treading down under our feet all reasoning about religion. And holy resolutions were kindled in our hearts as a fire which the Life kindled in us to serve the Lord while we had a being, and mightily did the Word of God grow amongst us, and the desires of many were after the Name of the Lord. O happy day ! O blessed day ! the memorial of which can never pass out of my mind. And thus the Lord, in short, did form us to be a people for His praise in our generations.—Abridged from the testimony of Francis Howgill at the beginning of the *Works* of Edward Burrough, 1672.

The Voyage of the " Woodhouse " (1657). This remarkable account of the voyage of the *Woodhouse*, in the summer of 1657, with the second party of Quaker " Publishers of Truth " bound for Massachusetts, shows the spirit in which the Quaker message was carried to America. Six of the party, with two other Friends, had made up the earlier mission, but the Massachusetts authorities, determined to protect the purity of their Calvinism, had imprisoned them under sentence of banishment for eleven weeks, and then shipped them back to England.

A true relation of the voyage undertaken by me, Robert Fowler [of Bridlington Quay, Yorkshire], with my small vessel called the *Woodhouse*, but performed by the Lord, like as He did Noah's Ark, wherein He shut up a few righteous persons and landed them safe, even at the hill Ararat.

The true discourse taken as followeth. This vessel was appointed for this service from the beginning, as I have often had it manifested unto me, that it was said within me several times :—" Thou hast her not for nothing " ; and also New England presented before me. And also, when she was finished and freighted and made to sea, contrary to my will [she] was brought to London, where, speaking touching this matter to Gerrard Roberts and others, they confirmed the matter in behalf of the Lord, that it must be so. Yet, entering into reasoning and letting in temptations and hardships, and the loss of my life, wife and children with the enjoyment of all earthly things, it brought me as low as the grave and laid me as one dead as to the things of God. But by His instrument George Fox was I refreshed and raised up again . . . [and] by the strength of God I was made willing to do His will. . . . Still was I assaulted with the enemy, who pressed from me my servants, so that for this long voyage we were but two men and three boys besides myself. . . . [After reaching the Downs], again reason entered upon me, and thoughts rose in me to have gone to the Admiral, and have made complaint for the want of my servants, and for a convoy, from which thing I was withholden by that Hand which was my helper. Shortly after the south wind blew a little hard, so that it caused us to put in at Portsmouth, where I was furnished with choice of men, according to one of the captain's words to me that I might have enough for money ; but he said my vessel was so small he would not go the voyage for her.

Certain days we lay there wherein the ministers of Christ were not idle, but went forth and gathered sticks and kindled a fire and left it burning ; also several Friends came on board and visited us, in which we were refreshed. . . . Also we met with three pretty large ships, which were for the

Newfoundland who did accompany us about fifty leagues, but might have done three hundred if they had not feared the [Dutch] men-of-war, but for escaping them they took to the northward and left us without hope of help as to the outward ; though, before our parting, it was showed to Humphrey Norton early in the morning that they were nigh unto us that sought our lives ; and he called unto me and told me, but said :—" Thus saith the Lord ; ye shall be carried away as in a mist." And presently we espied a great ship making up towards us, and the three great ships were much afraid, and tacked about with what speed they could ; in the very interim the Lord God fulfilled His promise, and struck our enemies in the face with a contrary wind, wonderfully to our refreshment. Then, upon our parting from these three ships, we were brought to ask counsel of the Lord and the word was from Him :—" Cut through and steer your straightest course and mind nothing but Me " ; unto which thing He much provoked us and caused us to meet together every day, and He Himself met with us, and manifested Himself largely unto us, so that by storms we were not prevented [from meeting] above three times in all our voyage. . . .

Thus it was all the voyage with the faithful, who were carried far above storms and tempests, that when the ship went either to the right hand or to the left, their hands joined all as one and did direct her way ; so that we have seen and said, we see the Lord leading our vessel even as it were a man leading a horse by the head, we regarding neither latitude nor longitude, but kept to our Line, which was and is our Leader, Guide and Rule ; but they that did failed.

Upon the last day of the Fifth Month [July] 1657, we made land. It was part of Long Island, far contrary to the expectations of the pilot. Furthermore, our drawing had been all the passage to keep to the southwards, until the evening before we made land, and then the word was :—" There is a lion in the way," unto which we gave, obedience, and said :—" Let them steer northwards until the day following." And soon after the middle of the day there was a drawing to meet together before our usual time ; and it was said that we may look abroad in the evening; and as we sat waiting upon the Lord they discovered the land. . . . Now to lay before you, in short the largeness of the wisdom, will and power of God, thus, this creek led us in between the Dutch plantation and Long Island, where the movings of some Friends were unto, which otherwise had been very difficult for them to have gotten to. . . . In that creek came a shallop to meet us, taking us to be strangers, we making our way with our boat : and they spoke English and informed us and also guided us along.

The power of the Lord fell much upon us and an irresistible word came unto us : That the seed in America shall be as the sand of the sea ; it was published in the ears of the brethren, which caused tears to break forth with fullness of joy ; so that presently for these places some prepared themselves, who were Robert Hodgson, Richard Doudney, Sarah Gibbons, Mary Weatherhead and Dorothy Waugh, who the next day were put safely ashore into the Dutch plantation called New Amsterdam [afterwards New York]. . . .

Robert and I had several days before seen in a vision the vessel in great danger ; the day following this it was fulfilled, there being a passage betwixt two lands, which is called by the name of Hellgate ; we lay very conveniently for a pilot, and into that place we came, and into it were forced, and over it were carried, which I never heard of any before that were : [there were] rocks many on both sides, so that I believe one yard's length would have endangered loss of both vessel and goods. Also there was a shoal of fish which pursued our vessel and followed her strangely and along close by our rudder, and in our meeting it was shown me, these fish are to thee a figure. Thus doth the prayers of the Churches proceed to the Lord for thee and the rest. Surely in our meeting did the thing run through me as oil and bid me much rejoice.—Bowden, *History of the Society of Friends in America*, 1850, vol. I, pp. 63-67.

Marmaduke Stevenson (died 1659), one of the Boston martyrs, who was hanged 27th October, 1659, wrote the following in Boston prison eight days before his death. At the end of 1658, the Massachusetts legislature, by a bare majority, enacted that every person of the cursed sect of

Quakers who was not an inhabitant of the colony but was found within its jurisdiction, should be apprehended without warrant by any constable and imprisoned, and on conviction as a Quaker should be banished upon pain of death, and that every inhabitant of the colony convicted of being a Quaker should be imprisoned for a month, and if obstinate in opinion should be banished on pain of death.

Some Friends were banished under this law, but in June, 1659, William Robinson, one of the party who crossed in the *Woodhouse*, and Marmaduke Stevenson, came into the colony " Boston's bloody laws to try." Mary Dyer of Rhode Island (see next extract) also came. The three Friends were banished, but returned, and in October Governor Endicott passed sentence of death upon them. The day of execution was Thursday, 27th October, the usual meeting day of the church in Boston.

When the Puritan lecture was over, the condemned Friends were taken to the gallows on Boston Common a mile distant. On the way the two young men began speaking, but the drums drowned their voices. " Yet they went on with great cheerfulness, as going to an everlasting wedding-feast." Being come to the ladder, they tenderly took leave of one another, then Robinson stepped up and told the people it was the day of their visitation, and desired them to mind the light within them, the light of Christ, his testimony for which he was going to seal with his blood. At this the Puritan minister shouted, " Hold thy tongue, thou art going to die with a lie in thy mouth." The rope was adjusted, and, as the executioner turned the condemned man off, he said with his dying breath, " I suffer for Christ, in whom I live and for whom I die." Then Stevenson stepped up the ladder and said, " Be it known unto all this day that we suffer not as evil-doers, but for conscience sake." He was turned off the gallows, saying, " This day shall we be at rest with the Lord." Mary Dyer also stepped up the ladder, her face was covered and the halter put round her neck, when the cry was raised, " Stop ! for she is reprieved."

She was again banished, but returned in May, 1660. Since her reprieve, others, both colonists and visiting Friends, had brought themselves within the capital penalty, but the authorities had not ventured to enforce it. After ten days, Endicott sent for her, and asked her if she were the same Mary Dyer who had been there before. On her avowing this, the death-sentence was passed and executed. After her death a member of the General Court uttered one of those bitter scoffs which prove the truest of all epitaphs, " She did hang as a flag for others to take example by." One other Friend, William Leddra, of Barbados, was martyred in March, 1661. Others lay in prison awaiting sentence, but were set at liberty, and a new law was passed substituting whipping out of the colony from town to town for the death penalty. Shortly after, the " King's Missive " (see Whittier's poem) reached Boston, and showed the royal disapproval of the policy of persecution. When the last Friend to be condemned to death (Wenlock Christison, afterwards released) had received his sentence, he had

said :—" Do not think to weary out the living God by taking away the lives
of His servants. What do you gain by it ? For the last man you put to
death, here are five come in his room. And if you have power to take my
life from me God can raise up the same principle of life in ten of His servants
and send them among you in my room."

In the beginning of the year 1655, I was at the plough in the
east parts of Yorkshire in Old England, near the place where my
outward being was ; and, as I walked after the plough, I was
filled with the love and presence of the living God, which did
ravish my heart when I felt it, for it did increase and abound in
me like a living stream, so did the life and love of God run
through me like precious ointment giving a pleasant smell,
which made me to stand still. And, as I stood a little still,
with my heart and mind stayed upon the Lord, the word of the
Lord came to me in a still, small voice, which I did hear perfectly,
saying to me in the secret of my heart and conscience, " I have
ordained thee a prophet unto the nations," and, at the hearing
of the word of the Lord, I was put to a stand, seeing that I was
but a child for such a weighty matter. So, at the time appointed,
Barbados was set before me, unto which I was required of the
Lord to go and leave my dear and loving wife and tender
children ; for the Lord said unto me, immediately by His Spirit,
that He would be as an husband to my wife and as a father to
my children, and they should not want in my absence, for He
would provide for them when I was gone. And I believed the
Lord would perform what He had spoken, because I was made
willing to give up myself to His work and service, to leave all
and follow Him, whose presence and life is with me, where I rest
in peace and quietness of spirit, with my dear brother [William
Robinson] under the shadow of His wings, who hath made us
willing to lay down our lives for His name's sake, if unmerciful
men be suffered to take them from us. And, if they do, we
know we shall have peace and rest with the Lord for ever in
His holy habitation, when they shall have torment night and day.

So, in obedience to the living God, I made preparation to
pass to Barbados in the Fourth month [June] 1658. So, after
some time that I had been on the said island in the service of

God, I heard that New England had made a law to put the servants of the living God to death if they returned after they were sentenced away, which did come near me at that time ; and, as I considered the thing and pondered it in my heart, immediately came the word of the Lord unto me, saying, " Thou knowest not but that thou mayst go thither."

But I kept this word in my heart and did not declare it to any until the time appointed. So, after that, a vessel was made ready for Rhode Island, which I passed in. So, after a little time that I had been there, visiting the seed which the Lord had blessed, the word of the Lord came to me, saying, " Go to Boston with thy brother William Robinson," and at His command I was obedient and gave up to His will, that so His work and service may be accomplished. For He had said unto me that He had a great work for me to do, which is now come to pass. And, for yielding obedience to and for obeying the voice and command of the everlasting God, which created heaven and earth and the fountains of waters, do I, with my dear brother, suffer outward bonds near unto death.

And this is given forth to be upon record, that all people may know who hear it, that we came not in our own wills but in the will of God.

Given forth by me, who am known to men by the name of Marmaduke Stevenson, but have a new name given me, which the world knows not of, written in the book of life.—Besse, *Sufferings*, 1753, vol. II, pp. 201, 202.

Mary Dyer (convinced 1654, died 1660), of Rhode Island, prior to her execution at Boston, New England, June, 1660, had been banished from Massachusetts, but returned and was sentenced to death with William Robinson and Marmaduke Stevenson. She was reprieved at the last moment, but in May, 1660, her dauntless spirit led her again into the " lions' den " of Boston, and this time there was no reprieve. See the note to the preceding extract.

Then Mary Dyer was brought forth, and with a band of soldiers led through the town, the drums being beaten before and behind her, and so continued that none might hear her speak all the way to the place of execution, which was about a mile. Thus guarded, she came to the gallows, and being gone up the ladder, some said to her, that, if she would return [home] she might come down and save her life. To which she replied, "Nay, I cannot, for in obedience to the will of the Lord I came, and in His will I abide faithful to death." . . . Then one mentioned that she should have said, she had been in Paradise. To which she answered, "Yea, I have been in Paradise these several days." . . . Thus Mary Dyer departed this life, a constant and faithful martyr of Christ, having been twice led to death, which the first time she expected with an entire resignation of mind to the will of God, and now suffered with Christian fortitude, being raised above the fear of death through a blessed hope and glorious assurance of eternal life and immortality.—Besse, *Sufferings*, 1753, vol. II, pp. 206, 207.

Katharine Evans (died 1692), was a prisoner with Sarah Chevers in the Inquisition at Malta, 1659-1662. Katharine Evans was the wife of John Evans, of English Batch, near Bath, who died in prison in 1664. She was a woman of indomitable courage, who had already penetrated into places closed against Quakers, such as the Isle of Wight and the Isle of Man. She had set out in 1659 for Alexandria and Jerusalem with her companion, Sarah Chevers, wife of Henry Chevers, of Slaughterford, in Wiltshire. They touched at Malta, then in the hands of the Knights of St. John. Here they landed and declared their message, though the English Consul warned them of the Inquisition. The next day they were taken and for over two years underwent terrible sufferings. At the end of 1661, Daniel Baker visited Malta, and offered to remain prisoner in their stead. English Friends, with the help of Lord d'Aubigny, a Roman Catholic priest, the Queen-Mother's Lord Almoner, at length secured their release, and they reached England about the end of 1662.

Oh, how may I do to set forth the fullness of God's love to our souls. No tongue can express it ; no heart can conceive it ; no mind can comprehend it. O the ravishment, the raptures, the glorious bright-shining countenance of the Lord our God ; which is our fullness in emptiness, our strength in weakness, our health in sickness, our life in death, our joy in sorrow, our peace in disquietness, our praise in heaviness, our power in all needs and necessities. He alone is a full God unto us, and to all that can trust in Him. He hath emptied us of ourselves, and hath unbottomed us of ourselves ; and hath wholly built us upon the sure foundation, the Rock of Ages, Christ Jesus the Light of the world, where neither the swelling seas, nor raging foaming waves, nor stormy winds, though they beat vehemently, can be able to remove us. . . .

I have been very sensible, dear husband, . . . of your sorrowful souls . . . for us. As being members of one body, Christ Jesus being our Head, we must needs suffer together that we may rejoice together. A true sorrow begets a true joy ; a true cross, a true crown. . . . The deeper the sorrow, the greater the joy ; the heavier the cross, the weightier the crown. —From letters to her husband, in Besse, *Sufferings*, 1753, vol. II, pp. 409, 412, 413.

Priscilla Cotton (convinced 1654, died 1664), was the wife of Arthur Cotton, of Plymouth. She was one of the first that received Friends in Plymouth in 1654, and was valiant for the Truth, suffering several imprisonments.

The Testimony of Priscilla Cotton to Friends, the day she died. . . . Friends, the cross is the power of God. When you flee the cross, you lose the power. That which pleaseth self is above the cross ; and that which pleaseth man is above the cross ; and that which shuns the cross yields to the carnal part and loses its dominion. Though the cross seems foolishness, stand in it ; . . . though it be a stumbling-block to the wise, stand in it ; there the dominion, authority and crown is received. And this is not for you to be exercised in only for a time, as at your first convincement ; but, daily, even to the death, as long as a desire, will or thought remaineth in you contrary to God's pure Light ; and judge by it ; and, as you wait in the Light, you will come to know a cross in the use of meat, drink and apparel ; and keep to the cross when alone or in company ; what the pure Mind of God stands against in you, that the cross is against.—*Piety Promoted*, Part III, 1706, p. 12.

Isaac Penington (1616-1679), the great Quaker mystic, the son of a prominent Parliamentarian leader, was already a man of forty-two, and a practised author when he joined the despised Quakers in 1658. He suffered five imprisonments at Aylesbury and one at Reading—some five years confinement in all, often in cold, damp and unhealthy rooms that nearly cost him his life. He was much occupied in writing, and in travail of soul, " being retired in spirit and mourning to my God, for the powerful bringing forth of His pure life yet more perfectly both in myself and others." His writings, though diffuse, are often strangely beautiful, and reflect his own depth of experience and tenderness of spirit.

I have been a man of sorrow and affliction from my childhood, feeling the want of the Lord and mourning after Him, separated by Him from the love, nature and spirit of this world, and turned in spirit towards Him almost ever since I could remember.

In this sense of my lost estate, I sought after the Lord, I read Scriptures, I watched over my own heart, I cried unto the Lord for what I felt the want of, I blessed His Name in what He mercifully did for me and bestowed on me, etc. . . .

But my Soul was not satisfied with what I met with, nor indeed could be, there being further quickenings and pressings in my spirit, after a more full, certain and satisfactory knowledge —even after the sense, sight and enjoyment of God as was testified in the Scriptures to have been felt and enjoyed in the former times. For I saw plainly that there was a stop of the streams and a great falling short of the power, life and glory which they partook of. We had not so the Spirit nor were so in the faith nor did so walk and live in God as they did. They were come to Mount Sion and the heavenly Jerusalem, etc., which we had hardly so much as the literal knowledge or apprehension what they were. So that I saw the whole course of religion among us was, for the most part, but a talk to what they felt, enjoyed, possessed and lived in. . . .

At last, after all my distresses, wanderings and sore travels, I met with some writings of this people called Quakers, which I cast a slight eye upon and disdained, as falling very short of that wisdom, light, life and power, which I had been longing for and searching after. . . . After a long time, I was invited to hear one of them, as I had been often, they in tender love pitying me and feeling my want of that which they possessed. . . . When I came, I felt the presence and power of the Most High among them, and words of truth from the Spirit of truth reaching to my heart and conscience, opening my state as in the presence of the Lord. Yea, I did not only feel words and demonstrations from without, but I felt the dead quickened, the seed raised ; insomuch as my heart, in the certainty of light and clearness of true sense, said :—" This is He ; this is He ; there is no other ; this is He whom I have waited for and sought after from my childhood, who was always near me, and had often begotten life in my heart, but I knew Him not distinctly, nor how to receive Him or dwell with Him." And then in this sense, in the melting and breakings of my spirit, was I given up to the Lord, to become His, both in waiting for the further revealing of His seed in me, and to serve Him in the life and power of His seed.

. . . But some may desire to know what I have at last met with. I answer, " I have met with the Seed."* Understand that word, and thou wilt be satisfied and inquire no further. I have met with my God, I have met with my Saviour, and He hath not been present with me without His salvation, but I have felt the healings drop upon my soul from under His wings. I have met with the true knowledge, the knowledge of life, the living knowledge, the knowledge which is life ; and this hath had the true virtue in it, which my soul hath rejoiced in, in the presence of the Lord. I have met with the seed's Father, and in the seed I have felt Him my Father ; there I have read His nature, His love, His compassions, His tenderness, which have melted, overcome and changed my heart before Him. I have met with the seed's faith, which hath done and doth that which the faith of man can never do. I have met with the true birth, with the birth which is heir of the kingdom and inherits the kingdom. I have met with the true spirit of prayer and supplication, wherein the Lord is prevailed with, and which draws from Him whatever the condition needs, the soul always looking up to Him in the will and in the time and way which is acceptable with Him. What shall I say ? I have met with the true peace, the true righteousness, the true holiness, the true

* By " Seed " the early Friends meant a part of the divine nature, capable of growth, which was brought into the heart of man.

rest of the soul, the everlasting habitation which the redeemed dwell in. And I know all these to be true in Him that is true, and am capable of no doubt, dispute or reasoning in my mind about them, it abiding there where it hath received the full assurance and satisfaction. And also I know very well and distinctly in spirit where the doubts and disputes are, and where the certainty and full assurance is, and, in the tender mercy of the Lord, am preserved out of the one and in the other.—*Relation of his spiritual travel*, written in Aylesbury Prison, 1667, and printed in Thomas Ellwood's *Testimony* at the beginning of Penington's *Works*, 1681 edition.

Everything in the Kingdom, every spiritual thing, refers to Christ and centres in Him. His nature, His virtue, His presence, His power, makes up all. Indeed He is all in all to a believer, only variously manifested and opened in the heart by the Spirit. He is the volume of the whole book, every leaf and line whereof speaks of Him and writes out Him in some or other of His sweet and beautiful lineaments. So that if I should yet speak further of other things . . . I should but speak further of His nature brought up, manifested and displaying itself in and through the creatures, by His turning the wheel of His life in their hearts. But my spirit hasteneth from words . . . [that it] may sink in spirit into the feeling of the life itself, and may learn what it is to enjoy it there and to be comprehended of it, and cease striving to know or comprehend concerning it.—*Some of the Mysteries of God's Kingdom glanced at*, 1663, printed in Penington's *Works*, 1681 edition, pp. 420, 421.

Robert Barclay (1648-1690). The first extract gives Robert Barclay's experience among other religious bodies expressed in the language natural to the thought of the age. This high-born Scotsman, author at the age of twenty-seven of the famous *Apology*, was the first to formulate Quakerism in a way which compelled the attention of the theologians of Europe. The *Apology* was a direct challenge to much of the Westminster Confession and the Shorter Catechism (1646-48), and, though decked out in abundant learning, and first published in Latin (1676), was the work of a man who felt that God " hath chosen a few despicable and unlearned instruments, as He did fishermen of old, to publish His pure and naked Truth, and to free it of these mists and fogs wherewith the clergy hath clouded it." The varied experiences which qualified him for his work are briefly given in the following extracts. His life had its full share of opposition and persecution, but its abiding inward peace filled it with calm strength.

My first education from my infancy up fell amongst the strictest sort of Calvinists, those of our country [Scotland] being generally acknowledged to be the severest of that sect. . . . I had scarce got out of my childhood when I was by the permission of Divine Providence cast among the company of Papists ; and my tender years and immature capacity not being able to withstand and resist the insinuations that were used to proselyte me to that way, I became quickly defiled with the pollutions thereof, and continued therein for a time, until it pleased God through His rich love and mercy to deliver me out of those snares and to give me a clear understanding of the evil of that way. In both these sects the reader may easily conceive that I had abundant occasion to receive impressions contrary to this principle of love herein treated of ; seeing the straitness of several of their doctrines, as well as their practice of persecution, do abundantly declare how opposite they are to Universal Love.

The time that intervened betwixt my forsaking of the Church of Rome and joining with [Friends], I kept myself free from joining with any sort of people, though I took liberty to hear several. And my converse was most with those that inveigh much against judging and such kind of severity, seeming to complain greatly for want of this Christian charity among all sects. Which latitude may perhaps be esteemed the other extreme opposite to the preciseness of these other sects, whereby I also received an opportunity to know what usually is pretended on that side likewise.—*Universal Love,* 1676, in *Works,* 1692 edition, p. 678.

Not by strength of arguments or by a particular disquisition of each doctrine and convincement of my understanding thereby came [I] to receive and bear witness of the Truth, but by being secretly reached by [the] Life. For, when I came into the silent assemblies of God's people, I felt a secret power among them, which touched my heart ; and as I gave way unto it I found the evil weakening in me and the good raised up ; and so I became thus knit and united unto them, hungering more and more after the increase of this power and life, whereby I might feel myself perfectly redeemed ; and indeed this is the surest way to become a Christian ; to whom afterwards the knowledge and understanding of principles will not be wanting, but will grow up so much as is needful as the natural fruit of this good root, and such a knowledge will not be barren nor unfruitful.— *Apology*, Proposition xi., sect. 7.

Elizabeth Stirredge (1634-1706), a Gloucestershire Friend, was a typical Mother in Israel of the early period of Quakerism.

I was in the nineteenth year of my age, when John Camm and John Audland came first to Bristol in the dread and power of the great God of heaven and earth, and I am a living witness that His powerful presence was with them, and made their ministry so dreadful that it pierced the hearts of thousands. O the dread and terror that seized upon my heart at the sound of John Audland's voice, and the sight of him, before I rightly understood what he said. But, before the meeting was over, the Spirit of the Lord moved in my heart, and in the Light I came to see my woeful and deplorable state, which made me to cry to God for mercy—a day never to be forgotten by me. And now I have arrived to the seven and fiftieth year of my age. O the many deliverances, both inward and outward, have I been made a living witness of. . . . How have the enemies roared, both inwardly and outwardly, and have come with open mouth to devour at once ? And how hath our God helped us ? . . . And now, my dear children, keep faithful to the Lord, . . . and your eyes shall see for yourselves as mine eyes have for myself. Be faithful to the motion of the Spirit of Christ Jesus in your own bosoms, and don't you overlook the little things, for they that be not faithful in a little shall never be made ruler over much. . . . Keep the Lord always in your remembrance, that you sin not against Him ; and remember to keep to the daily cross, which will crucify all the motions of the flesh, and keep you alive to God and near unto Him . . . and seek the kingdom of heaven and the righteousness thereof above all things in the world.—*Strength in Weakness*, 1772 edition, p. 162.

William Penn (**1644-1718**).   William Penn's life of high adventure, which has left its mark on the history of England and America, was the life of a man of commanding gifts, and eager spirit vowed, as the extract shows, to "follow the Christ, the King."   When he threw in his lot with Friends in 1667, he preferred "the reproach of Christ" to the career at Court open before him, and he never flinched from his decision.   His work as champion of religious liberty in England and founder of the "Holy Experiment" of Pennsylvania is well known, and, for his inner spirit, we can turn to his writings which rank high in the prose literature of the Restoration period, especially to *No Cross, No Crown*, and the two little books, called *Fruits of Solitude*, written when he was under the ban of the authorities owing to his friendship with the exiled James II.   Penn's other writings include his *Essay towards the Present and Future Peace of Europe*, written in 1693, foreshadowing a League of States.

What was [Christ's] cup He drank, and baptism He suffered? I answer : They were the denial and offering up of Himself by the eternal Spirit to the will of God, undergoing the tribulations of His life and agonies of His death upon the Cross, for man's salvation.   What is our cup and cross that we should drink and suffer ?   They are the denial and offering up of ourselves, by the same Spirit, to do or suffer the will of God for His service and glory, which is the true life and obedience of the cross of Jesus, narrow still, but before an unbeaten way.   For, when there was none to help, not one to open the seals, to give knowledge, to direct the course of poor man's recovery, He came in the greatness of His love and strength ; and, though clothed with the infirmities of a mortal man, being within fortified by the almightiness of an immortal God, He travelled through all the straits and difficulties of humanity, and, first of all others, trod the untrodden path to blessedness.

O come, let us follow Him, the most unwearied, the most victorious Captain of our Salvation !   To whom all the great Alexanders and mighty Caesars of the world are less than the poorest soldier of their camps could be to them.   True, they were all great princes of their kind, and conquerors too, but on very differing principles.   For Christ made Himself of no reputation to save mankind, but these plentifully ruined people to augment theirs. They vanquished others, not themselves ; Christ conquered self that ever vanquished them—of merit therefore the most excellent prince and conqueror. Besides they advanced their empire by rapine and blood, but He by suffering and persuasion. He never by compulsion, they always by force prevailed. Misery and slavery followed all their victories ; His brought greater freedom and felicity to those He overcame. In all they did they sought to please themselves ; in all He did He aimed to please His Father, who is God of Gods, King of Kings, and Lord of Lords.—Second (1682) edition of *No Cross, No Crown*, from *Works*, 1726 edition, vol. I, pp. 286, 287.

Thomas Ellwood (1639-1713). The extract gives an account of the early contact of the young Oxfordshire squire, Thomas Ellwood, with Friends about 1659. His persecution at home for refusing hat-honour to his father, the vivid account of his sufferings in London prisons, his intercourse with the blind poet Milton, his life-long friendship with Gulielma Springett, who became Penn's first wife, may all be read in his autobiography, published in 1714, and frequently reprinted, one of the most delightful of early Quaker journals. The editing of Fox's *Journal* was his greatest achievement, but his life was filled with countless kindly offices and unwearied literary work.

I had a desire to go to another meeting of the Quakers, and bid my father's man inquire if there was any in the country thereabouts. He thereupon told me he had heard at Isaac Penington's that there was to be a meeting at High Wycombe on Thursday next.

Thither therefore I went, though it was seven miles from me. And, that I might be rather thought to go out a-coursing than to a meeting, I let my greyhound run by my horse-side. . . . Being come to the house . . . I saw the people sitting together in an outer room, wherefore I stept in and sat down on the first void seat, the end of a bench just within the door, having my sword by my side and black clothes on, which drew some eyes upon me. It was not long ere one stood up and spake, whom I was afterwards well acquainted with (his name was Samuel Thornton), and what he spake was very suitable and of good service to me ; for it reached home, as if it had been directed to me.

As soon as ever the meeting was ended and the people began to rise, I, being next the door, stept out quickly, and, hastening to my inn, took horse immediately homewards ; and, so far as I remember, my having been gone was not taken notice of by my father.

This latter meeting was like the clinching of a nail, confirming and fastening in my mind those good principles which had sunk into me at the former. . . . The general trouble and confusion of mind which had for some days lain heavy upon me and pressed me down, without a distinct discovery of the particular cause for which it came, began now to wear off; and some glimmerings of light began to break forth in me, which let me see my inward state and condition towards God. . . . And now I saw that, although I had been in a great degree preserved from the common immoralities and gross pollutions of the world, yet the spirit of the world had hitherto ruled in me and led me into pride, flattery, vanity and superfluity, all which was naught. I found there were many plants growing in me which were not of the Heavenly Father's planting, and that all these, of whatever sort or kind they were or how specious soever they might appear, must be plucked up.

Now was all my former life reaped up, and my sins by degrees were set in order before me. And, though they looked not with so black a hue and so deep a dye as those of the lewdest sort of people did, yet I found that all sin . . . brought guilt, and, with and for guilt, condemnation on the soul that sinned. This I felt and was greatly bowed down under the sense thereof.

Now also did I receive a new law, an inward law superadded to the outward—the law of the spirit of life in Christ Jesus— which wrought in me against all evil, not only in deed and in word, but even in thought also, so that everything was brought to judgment and judgment passed upon all. So that I could not any longer go on in my former ways and course of life, for when I did judgment took hold upon me for it.

. . . So that here began to be a way cast up before me for me to walk in, a direct and plain way, so plain that a wayfaring man how weak and simple soever . . . could not err while he continued to walk in it ; the error coming in by his going out of it. And this way, with respect to me, I saw was that measure of Divine Light which was manifested in me, by which the evil of my doings, which I was to put away and to cease from, was discovered to me.—*History of the Life of Thomas Ellwood*, 1714 edition, p. 21, etc.

Thomas Story (died 1742), who lived about eighty years, came from the parish of Kirklinton, in Cumberland, and was an intimate friend of Penn. He spent some years in America and travelled extensively. The extracts are from the early pages of his elaborate *Journal.* He was a man of good education, designed by his father for a lawyer, and acquired an extensive knowledge of natural history. The *Journal,* however, is confined to his very wide and varied religious experiences. After composing the following " Song of Praise to the Saints in Zion," he was ready to destroy it, observing in it things written in the first person, which did not belong to his own spiritual state. But, since the matter had been set down as it came, and with undoubted evidence of the Divine presence, he preserved it, concluding it given by dictation from the Mind of Truth. It was true in itself, and might answer the states of many, and be his own experience in time, if he was faithful. The piece was written early in 1690, before he came into touch with Friends.

I was silent before the Lord, as a child not yet weaned ;
He put words in my mouth ;
And I sang forth His praise with an audible voice.

I called unto my God out of the great deep ;
He put on bowels of mercy, and had compassion on me ;
Because His love was infinite,
And His power without measure.

He called for my life, and I offered it as His footstool ;
But He gave it me as a prey,
With unspeakable addition.

He called for my will, and I resigned it at His call ;
But He returned me His own,
In token of His love.

He called for the world, and I laid it at His feet,
With the crowns thereof ;
I withheld them not at the beckoning of His hand.

But mark the benefit of exchange :
For He gave me, instead of earth, a Kingdom of eternal peace.
And, in lieu of the crowns of vanity,
A crown of glory.

.   .   .

He gave me joy, which no tongue can express,
And peace which passeth understanding. . . .

I begged Himself, and He gave me all.

He gave me power to do wonders also,
To keep His commandments, through His Holy Spirit,
And to walk in the paths of righteousness with joyful songs.

—Journal, 1747, pp. 20-22.

1691 : When we came to the meeting [at Broughton, Cumberland], being a little late, it was full gathered, and I went among the throng of the people on the forms, and sat still among them in that inward condition and mental retirement. And though one of their ministers, a stranger, began to speak to some points held by them . . . yet I took not much notice of it . . . my concern was much rather to know whether they were a people gathered under a sense of the enjoyment of the presence of God in their meetings, or, in other words, whether they worshipped the true and living God, in the life and nature of Christ, the Son of God, the true and only Saviour. And the Lord answered my desire according to the integrity of my heart.

For, not long after I had sat down among them, that heavenly and watery cloud overshadowing my mind brake into a sweet abounding shower of celestial rain, and the greatest part of the meeting was broken together, dissolved and comforted in the same divine and holy presence and influence of the true, holy and heavenly Lord, which was divers times repeated before the meeting ended. And, in the same way, by the same divine and holy power, I had been often favoured with before, when alone and when no eye but that of heaven beheld or any knew, but the Lord Himself, who in infinite mercy had been pleased to bestow so great a favour.

And, as the many small springs and streams descending into a proper place and forming a river become more deep and weighty, even so thus meeting with a people gathered of the living God into a sense of the enjoyment of His divine and living presence through that blessed and holy medium the Mind of Jesus Christ, the Son of God and Saviour of the world, I felt an increase of the same joy of the salvation of God, and the more by how much I now perceived I had been under the like mistake as the prophet of God of old ; but now [was] otherwise informed by a sure evidence and token, by the witness of the divine essential truth, in which no living soul can err or be mistaken or deceived, being self-evident and undeniable in all those who truly know Him.

Our joy was mutual and full, though in the efflux of many tears, . . . for the Friends there . . . did conclude I had been at that time and not before convinced . . . and their joy was as of heaven at the return of a penitent, and mine as the joy of salvation from God, in view of the work of the Lord so far carried on in the earth when I had thought not long before there had scarce been any true and living faith or knowledge of God in the world.

The meeting being ended, the Peace of God . . . remained as a holy canopy over my mind in a silence out of the reach of all words, and where no idea but the Word Himself can be conceived. But being invited together with the ministering Friend to the house of the ancient widow Hall, I went willingly with them ; but the sweet silence . . . still remaining I had nothing to say to any of them till He was pleased to draw the curtain and veil His presence, and then I found my mind pure and in a well bounded liberty of innocent conversation with them.—*Ibid.*, pp. 32, 33.

Samuel Bownas (1676-1753). The blacksmith apprentice, Samuel Bownas, whose widowed mother had a subsistence of less than five pounds a year, became one of the most powerful of Quaker ministers. He had a tall, comely and manly aspect and a strong, clear voice, and, though his schooling was small, became thoroughly versed in the Bible, and able by the force of its testimony to confront and confute gainsayers, and deliver his message to multitudes on both sides of the Atlantic. His *Journal* is an artless narrative of his sincere and hearty endeavours, as much as in him lay, to promote the doctrine of the Gospel of Christ in the earth.

Now to return to my apprenticeship, I had a very kind, loving master and mistress, and I had meat enough and work enough but had little consideration about religion nor any taste thereof. On First-days I frequented meetings and the greater part of my time I slept, but took no account of preaching nor received any other benefit, than being there kept me out of bad company, which indeed is a very great service to youth . . . but one First-day, being at meeting [at Brigflatts, near Sedbergh], a young woman named Anne Wilson was there and preached ; she was very zealous and fixing her eye upon me, she with a great zeal pointed her finger at me uttering these words with much power, viz. :—" A traditional Quaker ; thou comest to meeting as thou went from it, and goes from it as thou came to it but art no better for thy coming ; what wilt thou do in the end ? " This was so pat to my then condition that like Saul I was smitten to the ground as it might be said, but turning my thoughts inward in secret, I cried, " Lord, what shall I do to help it ? " And a voice as it were spoke in my heart, saying, " Look unto me, and I will help thee " ; and I found much comfort that made me shed abundance of tears. . . . I went home with a heavy heart, and could neither eat nor sleep as I used to do, but my work never succeeded better in my hands than it did at this time, nor my mind never less in it ; but my conduct as well as countenance was much altered, so that several in the family were doubtful that I should fall into a kind of melancholy distraction, but I longed for the meeting day and thought it a very long week. When the time of meeting came, my mind was soon fixed and staid upon God, and I found an uncommon enjoyment, that gave me great satisfaction, my understanding being opened and all the faculties of my mind so quick that I seemed another man, a divine and spiritual sweetness abiding with me night and day for some time; and I began to see and understand the Scriptures . . . plainly seeing a difference between a preacher of the letter and of the spirit. . . . And now the Scriptures and ministry from the openings of the Spirit seemed so clear and plain to my understanding that I wondered that anybody remained unconvinced. . . . I saw by experience wherein my shortness had been in being contented and easy with a form of truth and religion, which I had only by education, being brought up in plainness of both habit and speech; but all this though very good in its place, did not make me a true Christian; I was but a traditional Quaker, and that by education only and not from the Scriptures because they were a book sealed to me. And I now saw plainly that education though never so carefully administered would not do the work . . . there was no other way but this, viz., by the Spirit of Christ alone (John x. 1, 2, 3), to attain to true faith, which works by love and gives victory over our infirmities and evil deeds, working such a change in us that we can in truth from experience say we are born from above.—*Life and Travels*, 1756 edition, pp. 4-7.

John Woolman (1720-1772). In the spirit of universal love and of the pure wisdom given him by God, John Woolman, the lowly New Jersey tailor, set himself against slavery and social wrong, and the simplicity and purity of his *Journal* have carried the message of his life to the generations since. The extract that follows occurs during the English journey which ended with his death from smallpox at York, and gives expression to his experience of identification with the misery of the world and of being crucified with Christ. (For other extracts see Index.)

In a time of sickness, a little more than two years and a half ago, I was brought so near the gates of death that I forgot my name. Being then desirous to know who I was, I saw a mass of matter of a dull gloomy colour between the south and the east, and was informed that this mass was human beings in as great misery as they could be and live, and that I was mixed with them, and that henceforth I might not consider myself as a distinct or separate being. In this state I remained several hours. I then heard a soft, melodious voice, more pure and harmonious than any I had heard with my ears before ; I believed it was the voice of an angel who spake to the other angels ; the words were, " John Woolman is dead." I soon remembered that I was once John Woolman, and being assured that I was alive in the body, I greatly wondered what that heavenly voice could mean. I believed beyond doubting that it was the voice of an holy angel, but as yet it was a mystery to me.

I was then carried in spirit to the mines where poor oppressed people were digging rich treasures for those called Christians, and heard them blaspheme the name of Christ, at which I was grieved, for His name to me was precious. I was then informed that these heathens were told that those who oppressed them were the followers of Christ, and they said among themselves :— " If Christ directed them to use us in this sort, then Christ is a cruel tyrant."

All this time the song of the angel remained a mystery ; and in the morning my dear wife and some others coming to my bedside, I asked them if they knew who I was, and they telling me I was John Woolman, thought I was light-headed, for I told them not what the angel said, nor was I disposed to talk much to anyone, but was very desirous to get so deep that I might understand this mystery.

My tongue was often so dry that I could not speak till I had moved it about and gathered some moisture, and, as I lay still for a time, I at length felt a Divine power prepare my mouth that I could speak, and I then said :—" I am crucified with Christ, nevertheless I live, yet not I, but Christ liveth in me. And the life which I now live in the flesh, I live by the faith of the Son of God, who loved me and gave Himself for me." Then the mystery was opened, and I perceived there was joy in heaven over a sinner who had repented, and that the language, " John Woolman is dead," meant no more than the death of my own will.—*Journal*, New Century edition, 1900, pp. 237, 238.

Samuel Fothergill (1715-1772), came of Quaker stock in Wensley-dale, but for some years led a wayward and dissipated life. When he was twenty years old, his father set out on his third religious visit to America, and took leave of his son thus, " And now, son Samuel, farewell ! farewell ! and unless it be as a changed man, I cannot say that I have any wish ever to see thee again." The change recorded in the extract given took place shortly after. It is said that his father, on his return came late to a meeting at York, where he stood up and spoke, but presently stopped, saying that what he had to impart was given to another ; on this followed a powerful address from a younger Friend ; it was his son Samuel. Samuel Fothergill's travels were abundant, his ministry heart-searching and springing from freshly-renewed experiences. A visitor to a remote parish church in the Scilly Isles early in the next century, found a little volume of his discourses in weekly use ; one was read by the clerk, save on the infrequent visits of the minister.

Dear Friends : It hath lain heavy upon me for some time to write a few lines to you upon the following subject. The Lord Jesus Christ, in His everlasting kindness, that hath long strove with my soul, has been pleased to unstop my deaf ear, that I might hear Him the Shepherd of His flock, and to open my blind eyes and let me see my state as it really was, very desperate and very lamentable. He has shown me the dreadful precipice I was on the brink of, and breathed into me the breath of life. . . . He has set my sins in order before me, and shown me how far I had estranged myself from Him, raising strong desires in me to return to Him the Redeemer of my soul ; the considera-tion of which has raised in my heart a just abhorrence of my former practices that induces me to make this public declaration of them, which I desire to do in a few words.

I know my sins are so many, and so obvious to every one that it is impossible and needless to recount and remark upon them, for I was then as in the bond of iniquity, though it has pleased the Father of Mercies to bring me since into the very gall of bitterness, and into anxiety of soul inexpressible, yea, not to be apprehended by any but those who have trod the same path and drunk of the same cup ; yet, blessed be the name of God, He who hath kindled breathings in my soul after Him would sometimes break in upon me, and, though the waves of Jordan have gone over my head, His supporting arm was

underneath that I should not be discouraged.—Letter to the
Monthly Meeting, 1736, from *Memoirs of Samuel Fothergill*, by
George Crosfield, 2nd edition, 1857, p. 29.

Sarah (Lynes) Grubb (1773-1842), was the wife of John Grubb, of
Clonmel, Ireland, and afterwards of England.

At school I sought the Lord, feeling His power in my heart
operating against the evil propensities of my nature ; yet to
these corrupt inclinations I many, many times gave way ; and
for this I was brought under great condemnation, even as early
as when nine years old. . . . I went on sinning and repenting
for years ; still my love for good books increased, and for good
people. We had few books. The Bible and one or two
Journals of Friends are all that I can recollect reading ; and I
really valued them as highly as I was capable of doing in this
my childhood. When I grew to about thirteen years of age,
I began to discover something about me, or in my mind, like
the heavenly anointing for the ministry ; for the Lord had
revealed His word as a hammer and had broken the rock in
pieces in my living experience ; and I was contrited under
a sense of power and love ; saying even vocally when alone,
" Lord, make me a chosen vessel unto Thee." . . . With
respect to my first appearances [in ministry, when about seventeen years old] . . . I shrunk from it exceedingly ; and often
have I hesitated, and felt such a reluctance to it, that I have
suffered the meeting to break up without my having made the
sacrifice ; yea, when the word of life in a few words was like
a fire within me. . . . Much baptism and suffering was my
portion from time to time ; the great work of my salvation and
sanctification going on, while I was occasionally induced to
invite others to the needful acquaintance with Him who came
to redeem us from all iniquity. . . . It pleased the Lord to
call me into a path much untrodden, in my early travels as a
messenger of the Gospel, having to go into markets and to
declare the truth in the streets. . . . No one knows the depth
of my sufferings and the mortifying, yea, crucifying of my own
will, which I had to endure in this service ; yet I have to

acknowledge to the sufficiency of divine grace herein. . . . At Bath I had to go to the Pump Room and declare the truth to the gay people who resorted there. This was a time very relieving to my sorely exercised mind. In these days and years of my life I was seldom from under some heavy burden, so that I went greatly bowed down ; sometimes ready to say, " If it be thus with me, O Thou who hast given me a being, I pray Thee take away my life from me." . . . In the year 1801, I wrote thus : " O my heavenly Father, Thou hast seen me in the depth of tribulation, in my many journeyings and travels. . . . It was Thy power which supported me when no flesh could help, when man could not comprehend the depth of mine exercise. . . . Be Thou only and for ever exalted in, by and through Thy poor child, and let nothing be able to pluck me out of Thy hand."—*Address to her Children*, 1832, in *Letters*, 1864, p. 3, etc.

Elizabeth Fry (1780-1845), formerly Gurney, is well known for her great work in prison reform and other causes. She was one of the seven daughters of John Gurney of Earlham, near Norwich, and was known to her sisters as Betsy. The change in her life came when she was eighteen, through a visit to Norwich meeting by William Savery (1750-1845), of Philadelphia. The first extract gives Betsy Gurney's sister Richenda's account of this eventful day. Savery in his own *Journal* says, " I thought it the gayest meeting of Friends I ever sat in, and was grieved to see it. I expected to pass the meeting in silent suffering, but at length believed it most for my peace to express a little, and, through gracious condescension, was favoured to relieve my mind, and many were tendered." Betsy herself writes, " I wish the state of enthusiasm I am now in may last, for to-day I have felt that there is a God ; I have been devotional, and my mind has been led away from the follies that it is mostly wrapped up in."

" On that day [4th February, 1798] we seven sisters sat as usual in a row under the gallery ; I sat by Betsy ; William Savery was there ; we liked having Yearly Meeting Friends come to preach, it was a little change. Betsy was generally rather restless at meeting, and on this day I remember her very smart boots were a great amusement to me ; they were purple, laced with scarlet. At last, William Savery began to preach. His voice and manner were arresting and we all liked the sound. Her attention became fixed ; at last I saw her begin to weep, and she became a good deal agitated. As soon as Meeting was over, she begged my father to let her dine with William Savery at The Grove [her uncle's house, where the visitor was staying], to which he soon consented, though rather surprised by the request. We went home as usual, and for a wonder we wished to go again in the afternoon. I have not the same clear remembrance of this meeting, but the next scene that has fastened itself on my memory is our return home in the carriage. Betsy sat in the middle and astonished us all by the great feeling that she showed. She wept most of the way home. The next morning William Savery came to breakfast, and preached afterwards to our dear sister, prophesying of the high and important calling she would be led into. What she went through in her own mind I cannot say, but the results were most powerful and most evident. From that day her love of pleasure and of the world seemed gone." (Thomas Hodgkin, Swarthmore Lecture, 1911, *Human Progress and the Inward Light,* pp. 55-56 ; see also pp. 41-61.) In 1843, when suffering acutely from her last illness, Elizabeth Fry remarked to one of her daughters : " I can say one thing— since my heart was touched at seventeen years old, I believe I never have awakened from sleep, in sickness or in health, by day or by night, without my first waking thought being how best I might serve my Lord." (*Life,* by S. Corder, 1853, p. 601.) " My life has been one of great vicissitude : mine has been a hidden path, hidden from every human eye. I have had deep humiliations to pass through. I can truly say I have wandered in the wilderness in a solitary way, and found no city to dwell in ; and yet how wonderfully I have been sustained. I have passed through many and great dangers, many ways ; I have been tried with the applause of the world, and none know how great a trial that has been, and the deep humiliations of it ; and yet *I fully believe it is not nearly so dangerous as being made much of in religious society.* There is a snare even in religious unity, if we are not on the watch. I have sometimes felt that it was not so dangerous to be made much of in the world, as by those whom we think highly of in our own Society. The more I have been made

SPIRITUAL EXPERIENCES OF FRIENDS 45

much of by the world, the more I have been inwardly humbled."
She added, " I could often adopt the words of Sir Francis Bacon
—' When I have ascended before men, I have descended in
humiliation before God.' "—*The Gurneys of Earlham*, by
Augustus J. C. Hare, 1895, vol. II, pp. 195, 196.

Stephen Grellet (1773-1855) (Etienne de Grellet du Mabillier), the
preacher of Quakerism to Europe, and the inspirer of Elizabeth Fry's visits
to Newgate, had an experience that is one of the most remarkable in our
annals.   Born at Limoges, of a noble Roman Catholic family, he grew up in
frivolous society, embraced infidel opinions, and during the French Revolu-
tion fought for two years in the Army of the Princes.   Made a prisoner
of war, he escaped to Amsterdam, and after two years in Demerara, went to
the United States and settled in Long Island.   Prior to his contact with
Friends, and before the experience in 1795 at Newtown, Long Island, given
in the following extract, he had been suddenly arrested, while walking in
the fields, by what seemed to be an awful voice, proclaiming the words,
" Eternity, Eternity, Eternity ! "   It reached his soul, his whole man shook,
it brought him, like Saul, to the ground.   He remained almost whole days
and nights in prayer that the Lord would have mercy upon him.   In 1797,
at the age of twenty-four, he began his wonderful work as an evangelist,
carrying his living message through all grades of society and all parts of the
United States and Europe.

It was a memorable meeting—held in silence, however, as
usual—never to be forgotten.   Very soon after sitting down,
great was the awfulness and the reverence that came upon me.
It was succeeded by such a view and sense of my sinful life,
that I was like one crushed under the millstones.   My misery
was great ; my cry was not unlike that of Isaiah :—" Woe is me,
for I am undone ! "   The nearer I was then favoured to approach
to Him " who dwelleth in the light," the more I saw my unclean-
ness and my wretchedness.   But how can I set forth the fullness
of heavenly joy that filled me when the hope was again raised
that there was One, even He whom I had pierced, Jesus Christ,
the Redeemer, that was able to save me ?   I saw Him to be the
Lamb of God that taketh away the sins of the world, who was
delivered for our offences, and raised again for our justification ;
who is our propitiatory sacrifice, our advocate with the Father,
our intercessor with God.   I felt faith in His atoning blood

quickening my soul, giving me to believe that it was He who could wash me from my many pollutions, and deliver me from death and destruction, which I felt to be my just desert, for my many sins and transgressions. On my earnest petition being put up to Him, the language was proclaimed :—" Thy sins are forgiven ; thy iniquities are pardoned." Floods of tears of joy and gratitude gave vent to the fullness of my heart !

Then I thought I heard again a sweet language saying :—" Proclaim unto others what the Lord has done for thy soul." Apprehending that this was a requisition of *present* duty, I began to plead excuses, from the consciousness of my inability to perform the service. " Thou knowest, O Lord, that I cannot speak English so as to be understood," was my answer, " and what am I that I should proclaim Thy name."

There was not the least feeling then in me to flinch from doing or becoming whatever the Lord would require of me, but a sense of my inability and unworthiness. I have since seen that this was more to prepare me for a future day than a command for a present offering. My spirit continued so prostrated before the Lord and encircled with His love and presence, that I was insensible to what passed around me. The meeting concluded and the people retired, without my noticing it, till my brother, speaking to me, drew my attention, and I saw that we two only were left in the house. My gratitude was great when I found that my brother had partaken of the heavenly visitation. From that time he attended meetings diligently, and was a great comfort to me. But, during all that period, we had no intercourse with any of the members of the religious Society of Friends.—*Memoirs*, edited by Benjamin Seebohm, 1862, vol. I, pp. 20, 21.

Robert Charleton (**1809-1872**). This extract from the experience of Robert Charleton, of Bristol, has been chosen as typical of the message of powerful Quaker ministers in the middle of the last century.

That change of heart, which must be experienced by all who enter the kingdom of heaven, seems in his case to have been so gentle and gradual a process that no precise time can be named at which the love of his God and Saviour became the governing principle of his life. . . . He possessed a mind of considerable power and comprehensiveness ; and for many years a large portion of his time and strength was actively and zealously devoted to promoting most of the great philanthropic and religious movements of the day. . . . It was evidently the predominant desire of his heart to walk humbly with his God. His whole character and conversation plainly showed that faith wrought with his works and that by works faith was made perfect ; that he had purified his soul in obeying the truth unto unfeigned love of the brethren ; and that in watering others he was himself also watered.

Concerning his service as a minister of Christ, we believe it may with truth be said . . . that, whether he spoke of Christian doctrine, experience or practice, it was as one who had himself, in a spiritual sense, heard and seen, felt and handled, those things which he pressed upon the attention of others ; that the theme on which he most delighted to dwell was the love of God in Christ to our fallen race ; and that, while he assuredly believed and desired to uphold whatever is comprehended in " the faith once delivered to the saints," he evidently felt himself especially called to dwell upon the great Gospel truth that the Son of God did in very deed " bear our sins in His own body on the tree," and that His death was, in the fullest meaning of the words, " a propitiation for the sins of the whole world." How truly his manner of life harmonised with and adorned the doctrine which he preached, and how greatly this added weight to his ministry, is best known to those who had the largest opportunity for observing it.—Testimony of Bristol and Frenchay Monthly Meeting, in the *Yearly Meeting Proceedings*, 1873.

John Bright (1811-1889). The calm strength of John Bright's religious faith is illustrated by the extract given. In a speech at Birmingham at the end of 1865, he said :—" To the outward eye, monarchs and Parliaments seem to rule with an absolute and unquestioned sway, but—and I quote the words which one of our old Puritan poets has left for us—

'There is on earth a yet auguster thing,
Veiled though it be, than Parliament or King.

That auguster thing is the tribunal which God has set up in the consciences of men. It is before that tribunal that I am now permitted humbly to plead, and there is something in my heart—a small but exultant voice—which tells me I shall not plead in vain." It was this inward law he was always seeking to obey. In explaining his resignation from Gladstone's government in 1882, after the bombardment of Alexandria, he said :—" The House knows that for forty years at least I have endeavoured to teach my countrymen an opinion and doctrine which I hold, namely, that the moral law is intended not for individual life only, but for the life and practice of states in their dealing with one another. I think that in the present case there has been a manifest violation both of international law and of the moral law, and therefore it is impossible for me to give my support to it." John Bright's work as the champion of democratic freedom needs no recital here. Of the depth of his personal religion Lord Morley has said that the most impressive and pure piece of religion that he ever witnessed was John Bright reading a chapter of the Bible to his maid-servants shortly after his wife's death, in his beautiful and feeling voice, followed by the Quaker silence.

His deep sense of responsibility in the sight of God, and his intense human sympathy were the most powerful influences in drawing him from business into public life ; and his natural nervousness was thus overcome by his sympathetic nature taking up the cause of the poor and the wronged. Of his public speeches it might be said, he believed and therefore he spoke. His aim was not popularity or party triumph, but the hope of advancing the cause of Truth and Right so far as he saw it. With this in view, and under a sense of great responsibility, he frequently prepared his speeches with much care and solicitude, in order that neither the truth nor the consistency of what he said might afterwards be called in question.

Although at one time there were grave doubts in the minds of many Friends as to whether it was desirable for members of our Society to engage in active political life . . . it has been evident in John Bright's case that he entered upon it under a deep sense of duty, and that he endeavoured to carry his Christianity with him into all his public life. . . . All measures which he believed to be calculated to ameliorate the condition or elevate the character of the people . . . had the benefit of his earnest and powerful advocacy ; and this was sanctified and strengthened by the solemn sense of duty under which his services were rendered. The moral strength and moral courage of John Bright were markedly shown by his unflinching and consistent opposition to war and war-like preparations, which repeatedly cost him loss of popularity and severance from political friends.

His love and reverence for the Scriptures have been testified to by many who have known him more or less intimately ; and his serious and devout reading of the Bible in the family circle has frequently been spoken of, by those who have been privileged to be present, as exceedingly impressive and solemnising. It has been said that probably no other Member of Parliament could have introduced into his speeches in the House of Commons the deep religious sentiments and Scriptural quotations which he sometimes did, without provoking a sneer. But such illustrations coming from him were felt to be appropriate and suited to the occasion. . . . In his earlier years it was not usual with Friends to give much expression to their personal religious experiences and opinions—and our late friend fully shared in such reticence, which his own feelings of reverence and humility doubtless increased. But we feel assured that John Bright's simple, consistent life plainly indicated that his desire was to be a " good soldier of Jesus Christ," and to live under a reverent sense of divine guidance.—Testimony of Marsden Monthly Meeting, in the *Yearly Meeting Proceedings*, 1889.

John Greenleaf Whittier (1807-1892) passed his early years working on the farm at Haverhill, Massachusetts, where he was born, earning the money for his school fees by making slippers. Taking up work as a newspaper editor, he had thoughts of entering political life, but felt the call to devote himself to the cause of the abolition of slavery, though his strenuous advocacy of it involved unpopularity and sometimes great personal risk. In later life, when giving counsel to a fifteen-year-old lad, he said :—" My lad, if thou wouldst win success, join thyself to some unpopular but noble cause." His deep love of humanity found expression in his poems which were dear to John Bright and other reformers. The selections here given reveal something of the tenderness and richness of his own spiritual experiences. The strength of his appeal to the religious instinct of men, far beyond the boundaries of his own religious Society, is shown by the place which is held by his poetry in modern hymn-books.

In calm and cool and silence, once again
  I find my old accustomed place among
  My brethren, where, perchance, no human tongue
  Shall utter words ; where never hymn is sung,
  Nor deep-toned organ blown, nor censer swung ;
Nor dim light falling through the pictured pane !
There, syllabled by silence, let me hear
The still, small voice which reached the prophet's ear ;
  Read in my heart a still diviner law
  Than Israel's leader on his tables saw !

There let me strive with each besetting sin,
  Recall my wandering fancies, and restrain
  The sore disquiet of a restless brain ;
  And, as the path of duty is made plain,
May grace be given that I may walk therein,
  Not like the hireling, for his selfish gain,
With backward glances and reluctant tread,
Making a merit of his coward dread,
  But cheerful, in the light around me thrown,
Walking as one to pleasant service led ;
  Doing God's will as if it were my own,
  Yet trusting not in mine, but in His strength alone !
            —From *First-day Thoughts*, 1852.

I bow my forehead to the dust,
  I veil mine eyes for shame,
And urge, in trembling self-distrust,
  A prayer without a claim.

I see the wrong that round me lies,
  I feel the guilt within ;
I hear, with groan and travail-cries,
  The world confess its sin.

Yet, in the maddening maze of things,
  And tossed by storm and flood,
To one fixed trust my spirit clings ;
  I know that God is good !

I long for household voices gone,
  For vanished smiles I long;
But God hath led my dear ones on,
  And He can do no wrong.

I know not what the future hath
  Of marvel or surprise,
Assured alone that life and death
  His mercy underlies.

          .   .   .   .

No offering of my own I have,
  Nor works my faith to prove;
I can but give the gifts He gave,
  And plead His love for love.

And so beside the Silent Sea
  I wait the muffled oar;
No harm from Him can come to me
  On ocean or on shore.

I know not where His islands lift
  Their fronded palms in air;
I only know I cannot drift
  Beyond His love and care.

          .   .   .

—From *The Eternal Goodness.*

George Gillett (**1837-1893**) was a business man in London, who
wore himself out in staunch support of great moral causes.

From words that not unfrequently fell from George Gillett in
his ministry, we know that he passed through times of doubt
and darkness.

Near the close of one of a series of meetings at Holloway,
he spoke somewhat as follows:—" Over twenty years ago I
came under a deep conviction of sin. One day the burden
became so great that I could work no longer. I put away my
books, closed my desk, and left the office. I was walking down
Cheapside, when, in the rush and roar of London life, I was

enabled to put my hand by faith in the hand of my Saviour. My burden was taken away and my heart was filled with peace and joy in believing."—*Annual Monitor*, 1895, p. 72.

William Dent (1778-1861). This notice of William Dent, of Marr, is given to show the transforming power that may come from one quiet life.

The writer recalls in his school days the tall spare figure of a venerable Friend who regularly attended Yorkshire Quarterly Meetings. It was evident that he lived in the wholesome deliberate air of the country. His Quaker garb was spotlessly neat. His face spoke of indwelling light and peace with all mankind. When words came they were few and weighty. It is told how he would drive fourteen miles to a Friends' meeting to worship. On one such occasion he rose, and said, " God is love," and then sat down again. It is believed no listener forgot that sermon. He and his family were known to be of the salt of the earth ; but what could a plain tenant farmer accomplish in a small village aloof from the life of the world ? At the time when he settled in it, several of the houses were in an insanitary condition ; the labourers had no gardens to speak of, the children had no school, but there was a public house for the parents. When at fourscore years his call came to go up higher, he left a village where every cottage was a healthy home, where all able bodied labourers wishing for an allotment could have one. The public house had gone, and a good village school had been established. For many years the school-mistress had lived in his house. A Bible Society anniversary in his big barn was the annual festival and Eirenicon of the district. It may fairly be said that the whole neighbourhood was slowly uplifted by the coming of one quiet life into its midst.—Joshua Rowntree, Swarthmore Lecture, 1913, *Social Service : Its Place in the Society of Friends*, pp. 78, 79.

Joseph Bevan Braithwaite (1818-1905). Conveyancing barrister and Biblical scholar, Joseph Bevan Braithwaite, who found time for wide service in Europe and America as a minister, was a prominent leader of the Society of Friends for many years. The extract shows how it was the record of the lives of ministers who had finished their earthly course that won him to a life of loyal service to the Society of Friends.

Shortly after his arrival in London he was on the point of undergoing the rite of baptism and resigning his membership, " but," he writes, " I thought it only right to attend the Yearly Meeting [of 1840] throughout, and to form my own independent judgment. I well remember," he continues, " sitting with my cousin, George Stacey Gibson, on the further upper forms to the left of the Clerk's table. I listened with an open mind to all that passed, whilst I was at the same time writing a pamphlet explaining my views in opposition to Friends. The attendance of the Yearly Meeting deeply impressed me, and I was gradually brought to the conclusion that I must cast in my lot amongst Friends."

In a letter written to intimate friends at that time, he states, " I had been afraid that the scriptural doctrine of justification by faith in the blood of Jesus was not in deed and in truth recognised by the body of Friends. . . . But I heard the testimonies [concerning] deceased ministers, and was ashamed and self-condemned for my harsh judgment. . . . The enlarged and extended view which opened before me of the true Christian doctrine of the communication of the Holy Spirit to the mind of man, and of the accordance of Friends' views on worship and the ministry therewith, was the principal circumstance that weighed with me. I had been enabled, through unutterable mercy, to accept the Lord Jesus Christ as my Saviour ; now I saw somewhat of His unspeakable preciousness as ' the Good Shepherd ' and ' Counsellor ' of His people, ' always, even unto the end of the world.' " . . .

At the last sitting of the Yearly Meeting, J. B. Braithwaite made a public avowal of the change that had come over him, stating that he had been mistaken in the conception he had formed of the views of Friends, and that he wished to express his deep regret at the part he had taken in the late [Beaconite] controversy. " Sweet was the peace," he writes, " that flowed into my soul " after this avowal. Thus was it after several years of conflict that our friend's convictions became unalterably established, so that he could render unwavering allegiance and service for more than sixty years to the Society of which he was a member.—Testimony of Westminster and Longford Monthly Meeting, in the *Yearly Meeting Proceedings*, 1906.

John Wilhelm Rowntree (1868-1905). From 1893 to his death, twelve years later in his thirty-seventh year, John Wilhelm Rowntree, of York and Scalby, near Scarborough, with his wide vision of the message of Quakerism and his rich mental and spiritual equipment, was the prophet of a new era of life for the Society of Friends, and the inspiration of his life and writings is still powerful. He gained spiritual light, as hinted in the following extract, shortly before he found himself under the doom of coming and irreparable blindness. As he went out from the consultation into the street, and stood for a few moments by some railings to collect himself, he " suddenly felt the love of God wrap him about as though a visible presence enfolded him, and a joy filled him such as he had never known before." His last project was the planning of an adequate History of Quakerism, and he had already written three lectures on the rise of Quakerism in Yorkshire. It was in the spirit of the First Publishers of Truth that he desired Friends to go forward to their new tasks to-day.

It is a great mistake to think that faith is exclusively or even mainly an affair of the head. It is mainly an affair of the heart, a question of the spiritual temper or attitude of the soul. As William Law expresses it, in one of his essays, faith " is a living, working power of the mind, that wills, desires, and hopes and trusts and believes and obeys." Aye, *obeys*. That is where our faith is weak. That is where we need the potency of the Gospel. We know better than we do. Perceiving the good we continually choose the evil.

. . . I am, shall we say, the average man. . . . If anyone were to charge me with unorthodoxy, I should be painfully shocked. I read the Bible, perhaps sometimes wondering what I have read five minutes afterwards. I go certainly once, perhaps under favourable circumstances twice, to church, chapel or meeting. I don't understand what is meant by the Trinity or the Atonement ; I leave all that to the clergyman or the minister, but in a more or less definite way I believe that my earthly life is so irreproachable that my eternal future is sure to be pleasant. Christ, I say, is my Saviour, by which I mean (if I were ever so brutally frank with myself, which I am not) that He will leave me alone in this world and save me in the next.   So I go on.   Now and then someone upon whose companionship I depend is called beyond the grave.   On such occasions I am deeply touched. . . . And then the tide of life, business and pleasure flows in again.   The gap is filled. I forget and once more am satisfied to live on the surface.   I flutter through the hours like a butterfly in a meadow—dipping aimlessly now here, now there.   But let us suppose that the strong blow of some great catastrophe were to smite me. Something that destroyed the routine of self-pleasing and compelled me to face the realities which I have so steadfastly shirked.   Let it be some permanent physical restriction like blindness, or some financial disaster involving penury—no matter what.   Where do I stand now ? . . .   Everything is bitter, life and the interminable future are desolate.   Suddenly I realise that my Christ was a lay figure.   I made Him and draped Him myself.   I realise that at the heart of what I called my religion was but selfishness . . . and that my insincerity has brought upon me the doom of spiritual emptiness. . . .

But how are we to be saved ?   How are we to realise the Christ of our Gospel ? . . .   Beyond all question a first consideration is sincerity, the sincerity born for example of conviction for sin and the desire for pardon.   We must honestly seek the true life, we must honestly wish to escape the toils of self-love.   Assume this sincerity.   Assume for example that I have grown dissatisfied with a drifting life, that I have felt a touch of that satiety which is the scourge of the worldling. How, then, am I to set about the business of salvation ?   I turn to Christ, the Christ of the Gospels.   What is salvation by Christ ?   It is nothing mysterious, it is to be made like unto Him.   Again I quote from William Law : " . . . From morning to night to keep Jesus in thy Heart, long for Nothing, desire Nothing, hope for Nothing, but to have all that is within thee changed into the Spirit and Temper of the Holy Jesus.   Let this be thy Christianity, thy Church, and thy religion. . . ."

But we must know the *steps* of this pilgrim's progress. Let me state the case again in terms of personal experience.

I determine to seek this peace of God till I find it.   My sincerity is not to be doubted.   I am earnest in my quest.   So far so good.   I have the first condition requisite.   I am willing to pull down the prickly cactus-hedge of my sins.   I realise that self is the devil's workshop.   I want to get away from the prison of my selfishness.   I want to realise love.   But I am not going to do it by mere mortifications and penances. . . .   I am wrong in thinking that the Christian life consists merely in not doing things that other people do. . . .   Moreover, mortification of this sort breeds a judging temper and a spirit of pride. Self-sacrifice is self-realisation.   I must approach my holy experiment from another side.   I must seek not merely to lop off but to grow.   I must acquire something I have not got. And here is a difficulty.   In practical experience how am I to know what is meant by listening to the voice of Christ, obeying Him and following Him ? . . .   Conscience is a guide I can follow.   For example, be thoughtful of others, even in little things.   Make a practice of forgetting yourself.   In the past it was always *I*, what do they say and think of *me*, am *I* getting the recognition that is my due ?   Now let it be otherwise.   Am I helping him, what can I do for him, what am I thinking of him ? Am I giving him his due ? . . .   Someone angers me, insults me.   I want to hit back, sting with a sharp repartee, crush with a jibe.   I practise restraint.   I return soft answers.   And so I might illustrate at large. . . .

But I cannot rest satisfied here.   I seek not only discipline, but victory.   I want to know not only conscience but Christ. Yes, but to the sincere experimentalist, using his conscience as a guide, and seeking always to focus his life on that of Jesus Christ, as he knows Him in the Gospels, and recognises Him in His faithful disciples, there comes a time when the line between conscience and Christ grows very thin.   There comes a time when the higher life of which I am always aware, and which I have tried to follow, becomes so merged in my thought of Christ and my devotion to Him, that I can hardly distinguish the two in my mind.   There comes a time when suddenly I am on my knees, my whole soul flooded with light and love, tears in my heart and eyes, an unspeakable peace enfolding me. The pierced hands have reached through to me at last, and draw me gently forth to Him. " Come unto Me and rest," and I answer, " Yea, for I am hid with Christ in God."

I have sketched, you say, a hypothetical career. No, it is a story from real life. You say I have spoken in mystical language. I answer, Yes, the supreme moment cannot be defined in the dry language of theology, nor can words express it. You say the experience is the result of mental suggestion practised over a term of years. I answer, No one believes that who has once been there and taken off his shoes on holy ground—the reality is too overpowering, the effect too profound. . . .

But perhaps I have made haste too fast. If I go back to my pilgrim I find in his experience something upon which I have not touched. It is not a smooth progress that he makes. His sincerity wavers before the fierce resistance of hereditary evil, ingrained selfishness, natural sloth. There are times when he cannot keep his eyes upon the cross, when the goal upon which he set his heart grows dim, when the baser self yearns for the flesh-pots of Egypt. How can he win through ? There is only one way, the way of prayer. I do not mean formal praying, the rapid gabbling of the Lord's Prayer, or the set petition for outward benefits. I mean the prayer of the sinful man crying from the depths of his great need :—" Create in me a clean heart, O God, and renew a right spirit within me," the prayer of the longing soul seeking to escape from the clog of fleshly imperfection and to breathe the free, pure air of the spiritual life. . . .

Amid the feverish activities of these modern days, when the loud-voiced interests of the world stun the ear, may we seek by devotional exercise in the private sanctuary of the home, no less than in public worship, to realise the saving love of God. And, as we turn our thoughts inward to face the solemn realities of eternal life, may the light of God's holiness reveal our sin as He sees it, that, knowing our weakness, we may seek His strength, and pray the Father whom Jesus has shown us to take us as children by the hand, and lead us into His everlasting truth, by

5

the way of service and a life of love freely given.—*Essays and Addresses*, 1906, pp. 397-405.

Caroline Emelia Stephen (1835-1909), of Cambridge, sister of Judge Stephen and of Leslie Stephen, had been passing through a long period of inward questioning as to the fundamental truths of religion, her difficulties made greater by the dogmatic statements and assumptions which she found in the Church of England service. She came to know the power that sprang from " a deep quietness of heart and mind, a laying aside of all preoccupation with passing things . . . a resolute fixing of the heart upon that which is unchangeable and eternal."

I first found myself within reach of a Friends' meeting [1872], and, somewhat to my surprise, cordially made welcome to attend it. The invitation came at a moment of need, for I was beginning to feel with dismay that I might not much longer be able conscientiously to continue to join in the Church of England service ; not for want of appreciation of its unrivalled richness and beauty, but from doubts of the truth of its doctrines, combined with a growing recognition that to me it was as the armour of Saul in its elaboration, and in the sustained pitch of religious fervour for which it was meant to provide an utterance. . . . On one never-to-be-forgotten Sunday morning, I found myself one of a small company of silent worshippers, who were content to sit down together without words, that each one might feel after and draw near to the Divine Presence, unhindered at least, if not helped, by any human utterance. Utterance I knew was free, should the words be given ; and, before the meeting was over, a sentence or two were uttered in great simplicity by an old and apparently untaught man, rising in his place amongst the rest of us. I did not pay much attention to the words he spoke, and I have no recollection of their purport. My whole soul was filled with the unutterable peace of the undisturbed opportunity for communion with God, with the sense that at last I had found a place where I might, without the faintest suspicion of insincerity, join with others in simply seeking His presence. To sit down in silence could at least pledge me to nothing ; it might open to me (as it did that morning) the very gate of heaven. And, since that day, now more than seventeen years ago, Friends' meetings have indeed been to me the greatest of outward helps to a fuller and fuller entrance into the spirit from which they have sprung ; the place of the most soul-subduing, faith restoring, strengthening and peaceful communion, in feeding upon the bread of life, that I have ever known.—*Quaker Strongholds*, 1911 edition, pp. 2-5.

Lucy Anne Woodhead (1845-1912), of Manchester and Colwyn Bay, assisted for many years in the grocer's shop belonging to the family, and on retiring from business through ill-health moved to Colwyn Bay, choosing a house adjoining the Meeting House, so that she might serve the congregation as much as lay in her power during the declining years of her life.

Frequent attacks of bronchitis eventually compelled her to retire altogether from business and remove to Colwyn Bay, where she resided for the last seven years of her life. She purchased a house adjoining the Meeting House premises that she might be able to attend Meeting as regularly as possible, and she found what was perhaps the most important part of her life's work in the loving service she was enabled to render to the little congregation of Friends gathered there. One striking feature in her character was her great capacity for friendship ; her house was a centre from which was shed abroad sympathy with all sorts and conditions of men and women ; and to enumerate the tired souls in need of rest, and the impecunious unable to afford a holiday, to say nothing of Ministers visiting the Meeting, who were entertained in that hospitable home, would be impossible. . . .

A constant attender at Colwyn Bay Meeting writes :—

" Our little Patron Saint has passed from our sight. She had the manner of the *grande dame* and the heart of a child ; an infallible sense of humour, and no human being could be a gentler judge of another than she was. Her experience of life had not been a wide one, yet such was the intuitive power which love gave her, that it was never necessary to explain different standpoints, other modes of life ; she always understood and put the kindliest construction on it all. She dearly loved little children ; and though no child ever had the blessing of calling her mother, yet she mothered us all, and our Meeting. By devoting the last years of her life to our small gathering she gave it—a soul—and is there any higher form of creation than this ? She gave us a standard of what one might become who walked with God, and the younger generation, when in doubt, may be heard commenting, ' Miss Woodhead would not have said that.' To some of us she is closer in the Unseen World than she was in life, and the knowledge of her spirit's presence is a very present help in time of trouble."—*Annual Monitor*, 1914.

Thomas Hodgkin (**1831-1913**) banker and historian, wrote the following poem when he was in his thirty-seventh year. It carries with it something of the spiritual atmosphere of Thomas Hodgkin's life. After long years of varied service, the call came just as he would have wished, on a Sunday morning as he was preparing to start for meeting at Falmouth. There was no leave-taking. He had always dreaded a lingering illness or the loss of his reason, or any " struggle of this dying." " All his life he had been showing men the live-ableness of life, and then, quite suddenly, it was his turn to show them the die-ableness of death." There was no austerity in his life ; the keynote was joy. The following verses are from *Emori nolo : mortuum me esse nihil aestumo*, " Dying I abhor : I care nothing about being dead," a sentence translated and adopted by Cicero, in his Tusculan Disputations, i. 8, from Epicharmus, the Sicilian comic poet. Thomas Hodgkin wrote the verses on the Riviera in 1868.

F<small>ATHER</small> ! I live or die, in this confiding,
    That Thou art King ;
That each still star above me owns Thy guiding,
    Each wild bird's wing.

That Nature feels Thee, great unseen Accorder
    Of all her wheels,
That tokens manifest of Thy mightier order
    Her strife reveals.

And that without Thee not a wave is heaving
    Nor flake descends,
That all the giant powers of her conceiving
    Are Thy Son's friends.

Yet, I beseech Thee, send not these to light me
    Through the dark vale ;
They are so strong, so passionlessly mighty,
    And I so frail.

No ! let me gaze not on some sea far reaching
    Nor star-sprent sky,
But on a *Face* in which mine own, beseeching,
    May read reply.

    .   .   .   .

Such was my cry : hath not the mighty Maker
    Who gave me Christ,
Hath He not granted me a sweet Awaker
    For the last tryst ?

Given a Son who left the peace unbroken
    That reigns above,
That He might whisper God's great name unspoken
    The name of Love !

Have I not known Him ? Yes, and still am knowing,
    And more shall know ;
Have not His sweet eyes guided all my going,
    Wept with my woe ;

Gleamed a bright dawn-hope when the clouds of sadness
    Made my soul dim,
And looked their warning when an alien gladness
    Lured me from Him ?

Lord, when I tread this valley of our dying,
    Sharp cliffs between,
Where over all, *one* ghastly Shadow lying
    Fills the ravine.

    .   .   .   .

Oh, Son of Man, if Thee and not another
    I here have known,
If I may see Thee then, our First-born Brother,
    Upon Thy Throne ;

How stern soe'er, how terrible in brightness
        That dawn shall break,
I shall be satisfied with Thy dear likeness
        When I awake.

—*Life and Letters*, by Louise Creighton, 1917, pp. 427-429.
See also pp. 80, 81.

Possessors of Truth

Wherefore, O ye young men and women, look to the rock of
your fathers, choose the God of your fathers.   There is no other
God but He, no other light but His, no other grace but His,
nor Spirit but His, to convince you, quicken and comfort you,
to lead, guide and preserve you to God's everlasting kingdom.
So will you be possessors as well as professors of the truth,
embracing it not only by education but judgment and conviction,
from a sense begotten in your souls, through the operation of
the eternal Spirit and power of God in your hearts, by which
you may come to be the seed of Abraham through faith and the
circumcision not made with hands, and so heirs of the promise
made to the fathers of an incorruptible crown ; that, as I said
before, a generation you may be to God, holding up the
profession of the blessed truth in the life and power of it.

For formality in religion is nauseous to God and good men,
and the more so where any form or appearance has been new
and peculiar and begun and practised upon a principle with an
uncommon zeal and strictness.   Therefore I say for you to
fall flat and formal, and continue the profession without that
salt and savour by which it is come to obtain a good report
among men, is not to answer God's love nor your parents'
care nor the mind of truth in yourselves nor in those that are
without, who, though they will not obey the truth, have sight
and sense enough to see if they do that make a profession
of it. . . .

I shall conclude . . . with a few words to those that
are not of our communion. . . . The world talks of God,

but what do they do ? They pray for power but reject the principle in which it is. If you would know God, and worship and serve God as you should do, you must come to the means He has ordained and given for that purpose. Some seek it in books, some in learned men, but what they look for is *in themselves*, yet they overlook it. The voice is too still, the Seed too small, and the Light shineth in darkness. They are abroad and so cannot divide the spoil ; but the woman that lost her silver found it at home after she had lighted her candle and swept her house. Do you so too, and you shall find what Pilate wanted to know, viz., Truth.

The Light of Christ within, who is the Light of the World, and so a light to you that tells you the truth of your condition, leads all that take heed unto it out of darkness into God's marvellous light ; for light grows upon the obedient. It is sown for the righteous and their way is a shining light that shines forth more and more to the perfect day.

Wherefore, O friends, turn in, turn in, I beseech you. Where is the poison, there is the antidote ; there you want Christ and there you must find Him—and, blessed be God, there you may find Him. " Seek and ye shall find," I testify for God. But then you must seek aright, with your whole heart, as men that seek for their lives, yea, for their eternal lives, diligently, humbly, patiently, as those that can taste no pleasure, comfort or satisfaction in anything else unless you find Him whom your souls want and desire to know and love above all. O, it is a travail, a spiritual travail, let the carnal, profane world think and say as it will. And through this path you must walk to the City of God that has eternal foundations, if ever you will come there. . . . Here you will come to love God above all and your neighbours as yourselves. Nothing hurts, nothing harms, nothing makes afraid on this holy mountain : now you come to be Christ's indeed, for you are His in nature and spirit, and not your own.—William Penn's Preface to Fox's *Journal*, Bi-centenary edition, 1891, vol. I, pp. lvii.-lxi.

CHAPTER II

CONCERNING CREEDS

Vital Christianity consisteth not in words but in power; and however important it is that we have a right apprehension of the doctrines of the Gospel, this availeth not unless we are regenerated by the power of the Holy Ghost. We therefore tenderly entreat all to wait in humble faith for its quickening influence. . . . It may often be slow in its progress, but it is certain in its effects ; and, amongst the blessed consequences which it produces, we come to have an establishment in Christ, resulting not from any speculative system of belief, but from a heartfelt acquaintance with His power inwardly revealed to the soul.—From the *Yearly Meeting Epistle*, 1827.

In the seventeenth century, when the Quakers were often bitterly attacked for " heresy," they put out numerous statements as from the body of Friends collectively, showing that they were broadly in agreement with the historical Church of Christ in holding to what were regarded as essential doctrines—such as the Unity of the Father, Son and Holy Spirit ; the Divinity and Humanity of Christ ; the reality of Sin and the need for Salvation ; the resurrection of Christ and His redeeming work ; and the Inspiration of the Scriptures. This position our Society, speaking broadly, has always maintained, and has, therefore, claimed and still claims to be essentially orthodox and evangelical. We are in line with our fellow-Christians in the value which we, with them, attach to the historical facts on which our religion rests, and to the witness that has been borne to them through creeds, however far from final, and even through liturgy and symbol, though these to us are non-essential. But to us creeds have no value save as they testify to the eternal realities which men must apprehend by spiritual experience and express by life and conduct. A vital creed is not static but dynamic ; it can never be finally expressed in any form of words ; it depends upon and is held in the most intimate connection with the developing life of the Spirit in the souls of men.   Thus, while truth is eternal, our apprehension of it enlarges, and our expression of it changes, and Friends do not feel prepared to pin their adhesion to a form of words which at best embody a sincere attempt to define that measure of truth which has so far been apprehended in words appropriate to the age in which they are spoken.—From a statement presented to the Yearly Meeting, 1920, by the Commission appointed by the Yearly Meeting in connection with the World Conference on Faith and Order.

Chapter III

GENERAL DOCTRINAL STATEMENTS

Whereas many scandalous lies and slanders have been cast upon us, to render us odious, as that we do deny God and Jesus Christ and the Scriptures of Truth, etc. :—This is to inform you that all our books and declarations, which for these many years have been published to the world, do clearly testify the contrary. Yet notwithstanding, for your satisfaction, we do now plainly and sincerely declare :—

That we do own and believe in God, the only wise, omnipotent, and everlasting God, who is the Creator of all things both in heaven and in the earth, and the Preserver of all that He hath made ; who is God over all, blessed for ever ; to whom be all honour and glory, dominion, praise and thanksgiving, both now and for evermore ! And we do own and believe in Jesus Christ His beloved and only begotten Son, in whom He is well pleased ; who was conceived by the Holy Ghost and born of the Virgin Mary ; in whom we have redemption through His blood, even the forgiveness of sins ; who is the express image of the invisible God, the first-born of every creature ; by whom were all things created that are in heaven and that are in earth, visible and invisible, whether they be thrones, or dominions, or principalities, or powers ; all things were created by Him. And we do own and believe that He was made a sacrifice for sin, who knew no sin, neither was guile found in His mouth ; and that He was crucified for us in the flesh, without the gates of Jerusalem ; and that He was buried, and rose again the third day by the power of His Father, for our justification ; and we do believe that He ascended up into heaven, and now sitteth at the right hand of God. This Jesus, who was the foundation of the holy prophets and apostles, is our foundation ; and we do believe that there is no other foundation to be laid but that which is laid, even Christ Jesus ;

who, we believe, tasted death for every man, and shed His blood for all men, and is the propitiation for our sins, and not for ours only, but also for the sins of the whole world : according as John the Baptist testified of Him, when he said, " Behold, the Lamb of God, that taketh away the sins of the world " (John i. 29). We believe that He alone is our Redeemer and Saviour, even the Captain of our salvation (who saves us from sin, as well as from hell and the wrath to come, and destroys the devil and his works) ; who is the Seed of the woman that bruises the serpent's head, to wit, Christ Jesus, the Alpha and Omega, the First and the Last. That He is (as the Scriptures of Truth say of Him) our wisdom and righteousness, justification and redemption ; neither is there salvation in any other, for there is no other name under heaven given among men, whereby we may be saved. It is He alone who is the Shepherd and Bishop of our souls ; He it is who is our Prophet, whom Moses long since testified of, saying, " A Prophet shall the Lord your God raise up unto you of your brethren, like unto me ; Him shall ye hear in all things whatsoever He shall say unto you : and it shall come to pass that every soul that will not hear that Prophet shall be destroyed from among the people " (Acts iii. 22, 23). He it is that is now come, " and hath given us an understanding that we may know Him that is true." And He rules in our hearts by His law of love and of life, and makes us free from the law of sin and death. And we have no life but by Him ; for He is the quickening Spirit, the second Adam, the Lord from heaven, by whose blood we are cleansed, and our consciences sprinkled from dead works to serve the living God. And He is our Mediator, that makes peace and reconciliation between God offended and us offending ; He being the Oath of God, the new Covenant of light, life, grace, and peace, the Author and Finisher of our faith. Now this Lord Jesus Christ, the heavenly Man, the Emmanuel, God with us, we all own and believe in ; Him whom the high-priest raged against, and said He had spoken blasphemy ; whom the priests and the elders of the Jews took counsel together against, and put to death ; the same whom Judas betrayed for thirty pieces of silver, which the priests gave him as a reward for his treason, who also gave large money to the soldiers to broach an horrible lie—namely, that His disciples came and stole Him away by night whilst they slept.   And after He was risen from the dead, the history of the Acts of the Apostles sets forth how the chief priests and elders persecuted the disciples of this Jesus for preaching Christ and His resurrection.   This, we say, is that Lord Jesus Christ whom we own to be our life and salvation. . . .—Epistle addressed by George Fox and others to the Governor of Barbados in 1671, at the time of their visit to America (*Journal*, 1694 edn., pp. 358, 359.   Bi-centenary edn., 1891, vol. II, pp. 155, 156).

What then is [our] message ?   Words can but imperfectly express it, for life cannot be imprisoned in language ; the sincerest statement of belief is but an incomplete expression of truths which our spirits may realise, but which the mind can never wholly compass.   Our message can only be handed on from life to life ; yet we must endeavour to set forth in language the truth which we feel to flow through the very veins of our being.

We are called, as a Society and as individuals, to witness to the true meaning of the Real Presence of God in man.

Man is made to be the Temple of the Divine Presence ; but how is the building marred and broken ; how often has it been the haunt not of the pure spirit of love, but of base thoughts of pride, of lust, of selfishness.   Yet let us be thankful that, though the sanctuary has been defiled, though it may be buried beneath earthen masses which the years have only made greater, in the depths of every human heart there is a temple still.

Every man born into the world, be he who he may, has that within him by which he may come into personal communion with the Spirit of God.   He can never be at peace until this relation becomes a reality to him.   With Augustine our spirit's cry must surely be : " Thou hast made us unto Thyself, and our hearts are restless until they find their rest in Thee."

This life within our lives, which turns toward God, has been spoken of as the Seed.   The Seed was an image which

Jesus loved to use ; and it carries with it the thought of silent growth, and of the mysterious birth of the living plant from within the dead husk of the corn.

We must pass through this re-birth that we may enter into the heritage of the Kingdom ; and we need not only the birth, but the growth, if the fruit is to ripen. It is not given to us to understand how the new birth of the Spirit comes ; we feel the life-giving breath upon us, and the change that it has wrought.

But this we *do* know, that our spiritual life is rooted in God's love, revealed to us in the life, the death, and the rising again of Jesus of Nazareth. The food which our souls need is that life, spent for man in unselfish love, poured out for man in the passion of the Cross, triumphing for man in the Resurrection. He is at once the Revealer and the Redeemer, the supreme regenerator of human souls, the unveiler of the reality within us. He shows us what God is, what man *may* be, and, as we look up to Him, we begin to realise the meaning of good and the possibilities of life. Gazing upward thus, we see our own failure, our own wrong-doing, more clearly than ever before ; but we know, too, that the hand of the Healer is upon us, the life of Christ, outpoured for us, flows forth still ; over our darkness and death flows the boundless ocean of God's light and love.* This message of Divine love and life, revealing itself to us by sacrifice, is wider and greater than all our thoughts of it. The more we come to understand it, and the more fully it calls forth within us powers unknown to us before, the more we shall realise how poorly we express it in our words and in our lives, how much we have yet to learn of the Divine truth which is being ever revealed to us.

We shall pray that the life of each one may be made a sacrament, showing forth and handing on to others the light which Christ has revealed to us, the love which He has made real to us. Our thoughts will go out more and more to all our fellow-men, desiring in His spirit to share our brothers' burden, and to bring them into touch with Him who is the Way, the

* George Fox, 1647.

Truth, the Life, until they too feel that in Christ Jesus they can hear the beating of the Father's heart. . . .

Men to-day are waiting for the gospel of Divine Love worked out in human fellowship and in the freedom of perfect service. Such freedom, by which alone we can express to the full all that God would have us be, requires co-operation with each other; it means too the concentration of all our energies in the fulfilment of our ideal, and neither of these can come without sacrifice. This sacrifice is no reluctant gift, wrenched from us in spite of ourselves, no maiming or stunting of our nature, but the glad outpouring of our life for others, the free gift of our will to God and for our fellows. We are no longer our own, we are His and theirs.

> Our wills are ours, we know not how,
> Our wills are ours to make them Thine.*

Obedience to the Divine Presence in our lives brings with it the gradual remoulding of character, the upbuilding of life by life. It is not by abstract principles that the world is to be won, but by the transforming influence of personality. Words cannot explain the meaning of our message; it needs the definition of a devoted life. In such lives the old distinction of sacred and secular disappears as the whole nature is controlled by a common purpose, and the Divine Presence becomes the inspiring centre of action and of thought.—From the *Yearly Meeting Epistle*, 1907.

---

* Tennyson, *In Memoriam*.

CHAPTER IV

THE LIGHT OF CHRIST IN THE HEART

Shining Through All

Now the Lord God hath opened to me by His invisible power how that every man was enlightened by the divine Light of Christ; and I saw it shine through all; and that they that believed in it came out of condemnation and came to the Light of Life, and became the children of it; but they that hated it, and did not believe in it, were condemned by it, though they made a profession of Christ. This I saw in the pure openings of the Light, without the help of any man, neither did I then know where to find it in the Scriptures, though afterwards, searching the Scriptures, I found it. For I saw in that Light and Spirit which was before Scripture was given forth, and which led the holy men of God to give them forth, that all must come to that Spirit—if they would know God or Christ or the Scriptures aright—which they that gave them forth were led and taught by.—George Fox, 1648, *Journal*, 1694 edn., p. 22. Bi-centenary edition, 1891, vol. I, p. 34.

The Free Grace of God

And this I declare to all the inhabitants in England and all that dwell upon the earth, that God alone is the Teacher of His people and hath given to everyone a measure of grace, which is the light that comes from Christ, that checks and reproves for sin, in the secrets of the heart and conscience; and all that wait in that light which comes from Christ—which is the free grace of God—for the power of Jesus Christ to destroy sin and to guide them in obedience to the light, so shall they come to know the only true God and Father of Light, in Christ Jesus who is the Way to Him. And this I witness to all the sons of men, that the knowledge of eternal life I came not to by the letter of the Scripture nor hearing men speak of the Name of God. I came to the true knowledge of the Scripture and the eternal rest . . . by the inspiration of the Spirit of Jesus Christ.—William Dewsbury, 1655, *Works*, 1689, p. 54.

Return Home to Within

Now, therefore, everyone that thirsts, come unto Christ Jesus, who is near you, and wait to know his word in you, which is in the heart, which faith comes by the preaching of it in you, as you diligently wait and keep your minds unto it. And this, which shows you sin and evil, is in you, and makes manifest all that you have acted contrary unto it . . . and is the eye that sees the deceit in all its transforming in you ; and it will let you see. It hath often checked and called, but you have not answered its call, and so have chosen your own way, and so have gone from the way which is the light of Christ in you. . . . But now as ye return home to within, to the true light of Jesus . . . to be guided by it, you shall have true rest and peace. —Francis Howgill, *Works*, 1676, p. 46.

1656 : If you build upon anything or have confidence in anything which stands in time and is on this side eternity and [the] Being of beings, your foundation will be swept away, and night will come upon you, and all your gathered-in things and taken-on and imitated will all fail you. . . . Why gad you abroad ? Why trim you yourselves with the saints' words, when you are ignorant of the life ? Return, return to Him that is the first Love, and the first-born of every creature, who is the Light of the World. . . . Return home to within ; sweep your houses all, the groat is there, the little leaven is there, the grain of mustard-seed you will see, which the Kingdom of God is like . . . and here you will see your Teacher not removed into a corner, but present when you are upon your beds and about your labour, convincing, instructing, leading, correcting, judging and giving peace to all that love and follow Him. —Francis Howgill, *Ibid.*, pp. 70, 71.

A Measure of the same Love and Life

The divine mystery of this infinite God is revealed and discovered in the hearts of the sons of men whom He hath chosen; and He hath given us to enjoy and possess in us a measure of that fullness that is in Himself, even a measure of the same love and life, of the same mercy and power, and of the same divine nature. . . . These things ye know, if ye be born from above; and if the immortal birth live in you and you be constant in the faith, then are you heirs through it of the everlasting inheritance of eternal life . . . and all are yours because you are Christ's, and he is God's, and you have the Father and the Son.—Edward Burrough, 1660, *Works*, 1672, p. 698.

Christ Nigh to All

Glory to God forever! who hath chosen us a first-fruits to himself in this day wherein he is arisen to plead with the nations, and therefore hath sent us forth to preach this everlasting gospel unto all—Christ nigh to all, the light in all, the seed sown in the hearts of all—that men may come and apply their minds to it. And we rejoice that we have been made to lay down our wisdom and learning . . . and our carnal reasoning to learn of Jesus and sit down at the feet of Jesus, in our hearts, and hear him, who there makes all things manifest and reproves all things by his light (Eph. v. 13).—Robert Barclay, 1678, *Apology*, 1678, Propositions v. and vi., sect. 24.

An Effectual Witness

It is a distinguishing feature of the work of the Holy Spirit, that it bears an effectual witness to Christ, and brings to the enjoyment of His grace in those various relations in which He has been pleased to reveal Himself. Under the power of heart-searching conviction, it draws the believing soul, in contrition and humiliation, to the Saviour's feet. Here, through the acceptance of Him, in living faith, as the propitiation for sin, the reconciling love of God is shed abroad in the heart, and we are enabled to realise the inestimable privilege of access unto God ; not in our own right, or for any works of righteousness that we have done, but for the sake of Christ alone. In thus witnessing of Him, and establishing the soul upon Him, the Holy Spirit becomes a Comforter indeed. Through His sanctifying power the righteousness of God through faith is more and more manifested in the life and conversation, whilst all boasting is excluded. The promise of the New Covenant, in its most precious import, is fulfilled. The law of God becomes more and more plainly written upon the heart, whilst a yet clearer and clearer view is granted of the depth of that love which, in Christ Jesus, pardoneth iniquity, transgression and sin. Fervently do we desire that our dear Friends, everywhere, may press after an individual acquaintance with this heart-searching and heart-sanctifying knowledge of the Son of God. May none under the heavy weight of conviction stop short in the first stage of Christian experience ; but, yielding without reserve to the further manifestations of light and truth, may they be brought, from step to step in faith and faithfulness, to the full enjoyment in their own souls of the covenant of life and peace.—From the *Yearly Meeting Epistle*, 1857.

The Operations of the Spirit

As a Christian Church, we accept the immediate operations of the Spirit of God upon the heart in their inseparable connection with our risen and exalted Saviour. We disavow all professed spirituality that is divorced from faith in Jesus Christ of Nazareth, crucified for us without the gates of Jerusalem. One with the Father and with the Son, the Holy Spirit works for the regeneration of fallen and rebellious man. Not merely as the Enlightener of the conscience, and the Reprover for sin, is the Spirit mercifully granted, but also, in an especial manner, to testify of and to glorify the Saviour ; to apply, with sanctifying efficacy to the soul, His words and work when upon earth, and

His mediation and intercession for us in heaven. Hidden and often very gradual as may be the work of the Spirit, it produces a real and most effectual change ; and as obedience keeps pace with knowledge, the believer is privileged to receive more and more of the fullness which is in Christ. But let it never be forgotten that every increase of light and experience, how much soever connected with his usefulness to others, is also for the furtherance of the work in his own soul. He is taught by the Spirit to look unto Jesus ; that " beholding as in a glass the glory of the Lord," he may be " changed into the same image from glory to glory, even as by the Spirit of the Lord." To be guided by His Spirit is the practical application of the Christian religion.—From the *Yearly Meeting Epistles*, 1868, 1861, 1830.

He Died for All : The Light which Enlightens

The Lord Jesus died not for a favoured few only, but for all. " He is the propitiation for our sins, and not for ours only, but also for the sins of the whole world." His Church must ever testify to the unsearchable riches of His grace. The invitation is all-embracing. " Whosoever will, let him take the water of life freely." Firmly as we believe this truth, we think it right once more plainly to declare that we have never acknowledged any principle of spiritual light, life or holiness, inherent by nature in the mind or heart of man. We confess, with the apostle, that " we are by nature the children of wrath, even as others." It was under a deep impression of this great truth that George Fox writes,* " All are concluded under sin and shut up in unbelief, as I had been, that Jesus Christ might have the pre-eminence ; who enlightens, and gives grace, and faith and power." The light that shines into man's heart is not of man, and must ever be distinguished both from the conscience which it enlightens, and from the natural faculty of reason which, when unsubjected to its holy influences, is, in the things of God, very foolishness. As the eye is to the body, so is conscience to our inner nature, the organ by which we see ; and as both light and life are

* George Fox's *Journal*, 1694 edition, p. 8.

essential to sight in the natural eye, so conscience, as the inward eye, cannot see aright without the quickening and illumination of the Spirit of God. It is the capacity to receive this blessed influence which, in an especial manner, gives man pre-eminence above the beasts that perish ; which distinguishes him, in every nation and in every clime, as an object of the redeeming love of God, as a being not only intelligent, but responsible ; for whom the message of salvation through our crucified Redeemer is, under all possible circumstances, designed to be a " joyful sound."—From the *Yearly Meeting Epistle*, 1879.

The Light of God's Holy Spirit in the Human Soul

The main differences between ourselves and most other bodies of Christians arise from the emphasis we place on the Light of God's Holy Spirit in the human soul—potentially in all human souls, and known in actual experience as these are turned towards the Light and are obedient to it. This direct contact between the Spirit of Christ and the human spirit we are prepared to trust to, as the basis of our individual and corporate life.

From this source all our special " testimonies " flow. The Light of Christ in the soul may be experienced by all : no form of the Divine Grace is the monopoly of priestly caste, through whom alone it can be ministered to others ; all believers are called to be priests and in this as in all the service of the Church men and women are equally called to partake. Anyone may experience " the anointing," and, if this is known, may be called to minister to others of what God has given. We believe in the ministry as a spiritual service for God and men, free and open to any, whether men or women, who are truly followers of Christ, who know His Life in their souls, and hear His inward call. While the Life will necessarily find expression in some kind of human organisation, this must not be allowed to cramp the freedom of the Spirit. It is not the organisation, but the Life, that will safeguard the Christian community from error and schism. As the Light of Christ is known and followed, as men and women truly live their own life with God, they will be kept in unity with Him and with one another. Thus, in our church meetings and in our meetings for worship, we seek to rely entirely upon the actual presence and leadership of the Holy Spirit. We do not make arrangements for a " service," which will preclude the immediate guidance of the Spirit nor do we leave the public service in the hands of those ordained or set apart for it. Our experience, which we hold in trust for the whole Church, is that in meetings so held, i.e. in reliance on the presence and leadership of the Holy Spirit, the Holy Spirit does guide frequently in unexpected ways and to unexpected conclusions, and that such meetings can be held in an orderly way, under His leadership, to the profit of all, and to the furtherance of the work of the Church.

We are thus compelled at times to stand apart from other communions in such matters as a separated ministry, forms in public worship, and the use of outward sacraments. We feel that we must maintain our practice in these things as a vital part of our belief, as our testimony to the reality of the Spirit's presence with and guidance of our individual and corporate life. We do not make use of the outward rites of Baptism and the Lord's Supper, but we do believe in the inward experiences they symbolise. Our testimony is to the actuality of this experience even without the external rite.

So also the conviction that the Spirit of Christ dwells, potentially at least, in the souls of all men is the source of our refusal to take part in war, and of our opposition to slavery and oppression in every form. We believe that the primary Christian duty in relation to others is to appeal to " that of God " in them ; and therefore, any method of oppression or violence that renders such an appeal impossible must be set on one side. The life that flows out of the Christian experience must be a life of forgiving love, of purity and truth. The profession of a religious faith is valueless and even harmful if it is not constantly affecting life. The history of the Society of Friends does not show them as making any marked contribution to speculative theology, but rather as specialising in a type of conduct and corporate witness that they believe to be in harmony with the inward experience of God in the soul. . . . We believe that further applications of our belief to life and conduct will be revealed as we are loyal to Jesus Christ and obedient to His Light in our souls.—From a statement presented to the Yearly Meeting, 1920, by the Commission appointed by the Yearly Meeting in connection with the World Conference on Faith and Order.

A Word to All Who Seek Truth

We are living through a period when all forms of authority are being questioned. . . . Wherever we look, the ever-insistent child-spirit of the human race comes with its awkward questions, determined to examine things to their foundation and to know the truth. . . .

We have been content with ideas and expressions derived from the past, and have feared candidly to examine them in the light of the present day. We have often been more careful to preserve the old shell than to foster the growth of the living germ. Any such attitude is fatal. In particular, it produces that unreality, which, when once it creeps into religion, undermines the whole of our life and witness. No faith can satisfy that is not absolutely sincere and real and that cannot stand in the fierce light of truth.

We would welcome that light, from whatever quarter it comes, with all our hearts. We need the light if we are to get to reality. Men ask if there be indeed any ultimate reality, anything that can stand unshakable amidst the ruin of systems. To find the answer to this questioning is no mere matter of abstract interest, to every sincere seeker it is the deepest concern of life.

The very fact that men demand an answer to this questioning is part of the answer. If there is no ultimate truth, then the world is irrational, and they can have no trustworthy standard of truth and falsehood. The fact that all have such a standard is a witness to something beyond itself.

The man of science, following the demand for truth in himself, and guided by an inward criticism of what he finds in nature, discovers truth there. The joy of discovery is found in the correspondence between the inward sense and the outward fact.

So, in the sphere of ultimate truth with which religion deals, man has within him a sense of truth which we speak of as the Inward Light and which we believe to be of God. . . . That something we cannot call less than divine and universal for it links us with the eternal realities, and with our fellow-men of whatever race or creed. It may be hidden or warped by ignorance or pride or self-will or prejudice, but it cannot be wholly lost, for it is part of that which makes us essentially men—made in the divine image, and having within us boundless possibilities of life in God.

Our power to perceive the light of God is of all our powers the one which we need most to cultivate and develop. As exercise strengthens the body and education enlarges the mind, so the spiritual faculty within us grows as we use it in seeing and doing God's will. He who sincerely follows the light that he has, will be developing the spiritual eye and will be led with more and more certain steps towards the truth.

Thus understood, inward guidance does not mean unchecked individualism, for the follower of the light will be continually correcting his first perception of it by a fuller experience, and by that of others who have followed it more faithfully. Unity in diversity is thus achieved, because the light that guides the sincere and humble seeker is the light of God who is love. This is the path towards peace with all men, for there is no discord in the will of God. In His light we discover that He is at work in all others, and find unity with them in His love.

A religion based on truth must be progressive. Truth being so much greater than our conception of it, we should ever be making fresh discoveries. The mysteries of nature are continually being unveiled before the patience and perseverance of those who devotedly search them out and loyally follow the laws they discover.   So it is in the things of the Spirit.   A vista of infinite progress opens before us.

But what, in general, do we mean by progress ?   There may be movement, but, unless it is in the direction of conditions that are really worth having, it may be on a downward rather than on an upward grade. . . .   We believe that the insight which enables us to perceive a true standard of values and to aim at the things that are really worth while, is due to the same Light of God in our souls, which, as we have seen, leads us in the direction of truth.   Whether we recognise it as the Light of God or not, it is the condition of all true progress—above all of progress in the things of the spirit, which are supreme. " What shall it profit a man if he gain the whole world and lose his own soul ? " . . .

To-day, by life and word, it is our aim to call men back to the Light of God in their own souls, which, if they do but obey it, will lead them to the salvation that is in Jesus Christ.   This first-hand religion is what men need, and we testify to its power in our own lives, as in the lives of our forefathers in the faith. Far as we fall short even of our own ideal, it is for this we stand as a religious Society of Friends, seeking to show, by friendliness to enemy as well as to friend, by simplicity of life, by freedom from class or race or sex prejudice and dominance, that the spirit of Christ still has power in the world.

The life of the spirit must be a life of fearless adventure. Jesus dared to live in love with all men.   He lived as though the ideal were already realised.   Through Him we understand that God does not coerce men into goodness, because goodness cannot be gained that way, but that He seeks to win men to goodness by forgiving and self-sacrificing love.   To overcome evil only by good, to overcome error only by truth, to overcome hate only by love, always seems foolish and risky. . . .   Men fear to set sail upon an uncharted ocean, but it is just this venture that is characteristic of the Christian way of life, that constitutes the necessary challenge to the existing order, and that calls forth the heroism and devotion needed for its transformation.

—From a document entitled *A Word to all who seek Truth*, issued by the Yearly Meeting, 1920.

An Appeal to All Men

We appeal to all men to recognise the great spiritual force of love. . . . In spite of sacrifice and devotion, there is dissatisfaction and unrest in all lands. Consciously or unconsciously men are seeking for a new way of life. They cry for a bond which shall unite the world in freedom, righteousness and love ; that shall liberate it from its suffering, its hatreds, its disunion. They cry for a religion of life, for an active spirit of peace on earth, of goodwill to men.

Through the dark cloud of selfishness and materialism shines the Eternal Light of the Christ in man. It can never perish. This Light of Christ in the heart of every man is . . . the basis of our faith in the spiritual unity of all races and nations. Because we have been blind to this essential fact of life, we have failed in social and international relations, and are now in confusion. The profound need of our time is to realise the everlasting truth of the common Fatherhood of God—the Spirit of Love—and the oneness of the human race.

We have used the words of Christ, but we have not acted upon them. We have called ourselves by His name, but we have not lived in His Spirit. Nevertheless the Divine Seed is in all men. As men realise its presence and follow the light of Christ in their hearts they enter upon the right way of life, and receive power to overcome evil by good. Thus will be built the City of God.

We stretch out our hands in fellowship, sympathy and love, across frontiers, lands and seas. We call upon all men everywhere to unite in the service of healing the broken world, to bear one another's burdens, and so fulfil the Law of Christ.
—From a document issued by the Meeting for Sufferings 1919.

CHAPTER V

THE NATURE OF GOD AND HIS UNIVERSAL GRACE

We have met this year in the midst of the tragedy of war.
. . . In the darkness of universal sorrow and desolation we
cry for light. It seems to many that a God of Love could not
permit such terrible happenings. "They continually say unto
me : Where is thy God ? " (Ps. xlii. 3). We cannot give an
answer of strength and consolation to such a cry in terms of any
traditional faith. It is only as our faith is rediscovered and
resettled on a rock foundation that we can help a bewildered
world. We thank God that a new and living experience of His
power and purpose has come to us. Our hope is in this word :
God is Love—the power of God is the power of undying and
persistent love. It is through the hearts and minds and wills
of men and women that He works, and He waits for them to
open their hearts to love and to follow with unwavering
courage. In so far as men do this, they are helping to establish
the Kingdom of God and of His Christ—the rule of love in
the world. . . . They too must act as their Master acted in
unquestioning faith in the power of God's love and in the light
which lighteth every man in every nation, and to which we
can always make appeal. . . .

The world can only be won for Christ as men are possessed
by the infinite power which we call the love of God—the love
that will not let men go—the love that "beareth all things,
believeth all things, hopeth all things, endureth all things"
(1 Cor. xiii. 7), and that never faileth—the love that is Divine
Omnipotence.—From the *Yearly Meeting Epistle*, 1915.

It has been truly said of our Lord's human life that "for
the first time in history there appeared on earth One who

82

absolutely trusted the Unseen, who had utter confidence that Love was at the heart of all things, utter confidence also in the absolute Power of that absolute Love, and in the liberty of that Love to help Him " (D. S. Cairns, *Christianity and the Modern World*). Are we not often so fettered by the current conceptions of the universe, or by the spirit of unbelief in our own lives, that we lose that childlike expectancy which takes God for granted, and thus actually brings His infinite power into operation ? " In the last resort men think of God—the last factor in a situation ; for Jesus, God is the first factor."—T. R. Glover, Swarthmore Lecture, 1912, *The Nature and Purpose of a Christian Society*.

The spirit of the age is moving towards a belief in God as a pervading influence. We need to recapture the vivid sense of Him as a free agent in His own world, ever at liberty to help men. Jesus Christ had that sense, and, as He dwells within us, He can bring it to us. That is just what He has done for all the great pioneers in the spiritual history of mankind, and for multitudes of ordinary men and women.—From the *Yearly Meeting Epistle*, 1912.

How can we gain [a] new spirit ? How can we break loose from our fears and suspicions and from the grip of complacent materialism, and face the issues with new faith in God and man ?

Only by a fresh sense of the presence and character of God.

He has been defined in words that make Him an unreal abstraction ; crude human passions have been associated with His nature ; He has been presented to men as the authority upholding national ambitions or class or ecclesiastical tyrannies ; in one or other of these ways His nature has too often been kept out of our lives, or we have even presumed to implicate His name in the evils of our so-called Christian civilisation. But, if we feel our need of Him, and sincerely want to know His reign and will and nature, and are willing to let them re-mould our lives and heal the diseases of our world-order, we can turn away from these unsatisfying notions and see Him for ourselves —so far at least as here on earth we can see the fullness of God. There is one who has not only seen Him but has lived Him out in His own life, the man Jesus. God is like Jesus Christ, and we can rule out of our thoughts of Him everything that conflicts with the character of Christ. " He that hath seen Me hath seen the Father " (John xiv. 9).

Jesus was the man of the people, who knew their joys and sorrows because He lived as one of them. He learnt life at the carpenter's bench in Nazareth. He knew the trouble His mother had in patching the old garment, the value of the woman's lost coin, the cost to the widow of her two mites, the difficulty of the poor woman in getting justice from the unjust judge. He took our common life and daily toil and made them into divine things. The crowded cities of Galilee were His home. His heart went out to the helpless and the diseased, to the oppressed poor, to the rich, starved of true fellowship, and to the self-righteous, separated by their hardness of heart from their fellows and from God. He gave Himself to men without reserve, in loving fellowship ; their life and lot came into His life ; those who opened their hearts to Him knew His life ; and overcoming love came into their lives. When His people refused Him, and crucified Him, His love still sought them undespairing.

This is how Jesus lived and died, and still lives on among men.

This is how God lives among men.

This is how we are to live among men.

In our hearts we must know this life of unity with God and our fellows, and we must then, from our hearts, live it out as God's way of life for the world. It will open our eyes to the oppression caused by many of the economic and other privileges which we have often taken for granted, and in opening our eyes will abase our hearts. It will send us forth to break down the social and educational barriers and to abolish the servitudes, which mar the fellowship of the human family. It will take us with Jesus not only into lowly service but also into clear-sighted truth. We shall find our lives brought alongside the lives of others in practical fellowship. We may have to give up what the world counts most dear, but we shall be lifted into the joy of love. Our feet will be beautiful with reconciliation as we go in and out among men with the gospel of peace.

Dare we live above possessions and passions in this way of discipleship, in sincere comradeship with Jesus and with mankind ? Dare we see Him as He is, and leave all in order to follow as He shall lead us ? Dare we rely to the uttermost, as He did, on the fact of the love of God ? If we take into our hearts His love and His way of life, and live them out in our relationships—industrial, social, international, inter-racial—then indeed we may go forward, in the courage of quietness, to the joyful adventure of establishing that commonwealth, glorious beyond man's dreams, which Jesus proclaimed as the reign of God upon earth.

To each of us, however small our opportunities may seem, some part of God's work will be given to do, a part greater than our fears or even than our present faith. We shall find that our hearts are made strong in prayer and joyful in praise, our eyes are kindled to see the truth, our feet can go on God's embassies, our hands can help to heal, our lips and lives can speak His love. And, through us, men in their need may again see God in the face of Jesus Christ.—From the *Yearly Meeting Epistle*, 1920.

CHAPTER VI

THE PERSON AND WORK OF JESUS CHRIST

Christ Human and Divine

The New Testament clearly sets out Christ as fully human and as fully divine. The writers are conscious of no difficulty or contradiction involved in this position. It seemed to them the most natural thing in the world. Probably the sense of contradiction only arises in our minds through ignorance of what is meant by personality. We have set divinity over against humanity, on the assumption that so much added to the one must be so much subtracted from the other. Some have so emphasised Christ's divinity as to leave no room for His humanity, while others have done just the reverse. It seems so easy to solve the problem by cutting the knot; either say that Christ was absolute God, or that he was ordinary man. But this does not solve the problem, for either solution fails to take account of many of the facts. The difficulty is to get a conception of Jesus that is true to all the facts—of one who was the Incarnate Son of God and yet (perhaps we should say " and *therefore* ") was truly man. It is a pity that we insist on using the terms " humanity " and " divinity " as though they implied opposition. May we not rather say that Jesus " shows us the divine life humanly lived and the human life divinely lived ? " But of one thing we can be certain—there are depths beneath depths, and heights above heights in the personality of Jesus which make rash generalisations or superficial solutions absurd. We are standing before the greatest character in history and we may well hesitate before trying to express Him in a formula.—Statement prepared by Yorkshire Quarterly Meeting, 1919, and printed in the *Yearly Meeting Proceedings*, 1919.

Christ Within and the Christ of History

Christ is not divided ; the Christ who dwells within, the hope of glory, is the Christ of history. Only as we follow the guidance of the Holy Spirit and by faith embrace the Lord Jesus as the Redeemer of the world, and as our personal Saviour, can we hope to perform an adequate part in the social and other service which lies before us ; for, after all, the world's misery is the result of the world's sin. War, intemperance, avarice, lust, the chief sources of suffering and poverty, are the outcome of selfishness ; and all selfishness is sin. Civilisation makes but small progress against its ravages. We need a fresh vision of the cross of Christ. Coming as penitents to the foot of that cross, we find pardon, peace and power. . . . Christ's life is the key to our life, and His service the key to our service. Underlying all difference of view, is the reality of the power of the living Christ, whose love goes deeper than all our experience. By grace may it be given to us humbly and gratefully to confess : " The life which I now live in the flesh I live by the faith of the Son of God, who loved me and gave Himself for me " (Gal. ii. 20).—From the *Yearly Meeting Epistle*, 1906.

Christ the Life

In the afternoon the people gathered about me, with several of their preachers ; it was judged there were above a thousand people ; amongst whom I declared God's everlasting truth and word of life freely and largely, for about the space of three hours, directing all to the Spirit of God in themselves ; that they might be turned from the darkness to the light, and believe in it, that they might become the children of it ; and might be turned from the power of Satan, which they had been under, unto God ; and by the Spirit of Truth might be led into all truth, and sensibly understand the words of the prophets and of Christ and of the apostles ; and might all come to know Christ to be their Teacher to instruct them, their Counsellor to direct them, their Shepherd to feed them, their Bishop to oversee them, and their Prophet to open divine mysteries to them ; and might know their bodies to be prepared, sanctified and made fit temples for God and Christ to dwell in.   And, in the openings of the heavenly life, I opened unto them the prophets and the figures and shadows and directed them to Christ the Substance.—George Fox's sermon on Firbank Fell, near Sedbergh, Whitsuntide, 1652, *Journal*, 1694 edition, pp. 74, 75.   Bi-centenary edition, 1891, vol. I, p. 113.

The Place of Christ

The Son of God is to be heard in all things, who is the Saviour and the Redeemer, and hath laid down His life and bought His sheep with His precious blood.

And we can challenge all the world.   Who hath anything to say against our Way, our Saviour, our Redeemer, who is our Prophet, whom God hath raised up that we may hear, and whom we must hear in all things ?   Who hath anything against our Shepherd, Christ Jesus, who leads and feeds us, and we know His heavenly voice ?   And who hath anything against our Bishop, in whose mouth was never guile found, who doth oversee us in His pasture of life, that we do not go astray from God and out of His fold ?   And who hath anything against our Priest, Christ Jesus, made higher than the heavens, who gives us freely and commands us to give freely ?   And who hath anything to say against our Leader and Counsellor, Christ Jesus, who never sinned, but is holy and harmless and separate from sinners ?   God hath commanded us to hear Him ; and He saith : " Learn of Me."—George Fox's Sermon at Bristol, 1673, on his return from America, *Journal*, 1694 edition, p. 385.   Bi-centenary edition, 1891, vol. II, p. 200.

The Work of Jesus Christ

In order that, as we have received Christ, so we may walk in Him in all holiness and godliness of conversation, we earnestly exhort that ye hold fast the profession of the faith of our Lord Jesus Christ without wavering ; both in respect to His outward coming in the flesh, His sufferings, death, resurrection, ascension,

mediation and intercession at the right hand of the Father ; and
to the inward manifestation of His grace and Holy Spirit in our
hearts powerfully working in the soul of man to the subduing
of every evil affection and lust, and to the purifying of our consciences from dead works to serve the living God ; and that
through the virtue and efficacy of this most holy faith, ye may
become strong in the Lord and in the power of His might.—From
the *Yearly Meeting Epistle*, 1736.

We feel ourselves called upon, at this time, to avow our
belief in the inspiration and divine authority of the Old and New
Testament.

We further believe that the promise made after the transgression of our first parents, in the consequence of whose fall
all the posterity of Adam are involved, that the seed of the
woman shall bruise the head of the serpent ; and the declaration
unto Abraham, " In thy seed shall all the nations of the earth
be blessed," had a direct reference to the coming in the flesh of
the Lord Jesus Christ. To Him also did the prophet Isaiah
bear testimony when he declared, " Unto us a child is born,
unto us a son is given : and the government shall be upon his
shoulder : and his name shall be called wonderful Counsellor,
the mighty God, the everlasting Father, the Prince of Peace.
Of the increase of his government and peace there shall be no
end." And again, the same prophet spoke of Him when he
said, " Surely he hath borne our griefs and carried our sorrows :
yet we did esteem him stricken, smitten of God, and afflicted ;
but he was wounded for our transgressions, he was bruised for
our iniquities ; the chastisement of our peace was upon him ;
and with his stripes we are healed." The same blessed
Redeemer is emphatically denominated by the prophet Jeremiah,
the Lord our Righteousness.

At that period, and in that miraculous manner, which God
in His perfect wisdom saw fit, the promised Messiah appeared
personally upon earth, when " He took not on Him the nature
of angels ; but He took on Him the Seed of Abraham." He
" was in all points tempted like as we are, yet without sin."
Having finished the work which was given Him to do, He gave

7

Himself for us an offering and a sacrifice to God. He tasted death for every man. " He is the propitiation for our sins ; and not for ours only, but also for the sins of the whole world." " We have redemption through His blood, even the forgiveness of sins." He passed into the heavens ; and being the brightness of the glory of God, " and the express image of His person, and upholding all things by the word of His power, when He had by Himself purged our sins, sat down on the right hand of the Majesty on high " ; and " ever liveth to make intercession for us."

It is by the Lord Jesus Christ that the world will be judged in righteousness. He is " the mediator of the new covenant " ; —" the image of the invisible God, the first-born of every creature : for by Him were all things created that are in heaven and that are in earth, visible and invisible, whether they be thrones, or dominions, or principalities or powers : all things were created by Him, and for Him : and He is before all things, and by Him all things consist." " In Him dwelleth all the fullness of the Godhead bodily " ; and to Him did the Evangelist bear testimony when he said, " In the beginning was the Word, and the Word was with God, and the Word was God. The same was in the beginning with God. All things were made by Him; and without Him was not anything made that was made. In Him was life ; and the life was the light of men." He " Was the true light, which lighteth every man that cometh into the world."

Our blessed Lord Himself spoke of His perpetual dominion and power in His Church, when He said, " My sheep hear my voice, and I know them, and they follow me ; and I give unto them eternal life " ; and when, describing the spiritual food which He bestoweth on the true believers, He declared, " I am the bread of life : he that cometh to me shall never hunger, and he that believeth on me shall never thirst." He spoke also of His saving grace, bestowed on those who come in faith unto Him, when He said, " Whosoever drinketh of the water that I shall give him shall never thirst ; but the water that I shall give him shall be in him a well of water, springing up into everlasting life."

Our religious Society, from its earliest establishment to the present day, has received these most important doctrines of Holy Scripture in their plain and obvious acceptation . . . and it is the earnest desire of this Meeting that all who profess our name may so live and so walk before God as that they may know these sacred truths to be blessed to them individually. We desire that, as the mere profession of sound Christian doctrine will not avail to the salvation of the soul, all may attain to a living efficacious faith, which through the power of the Holy Ghost bringeth forth fruit unto holiness ; the end whereof is everlasting life through Jesus Christ our Lord. " Blessing and honour, and glory, and power, be unto Him that sitteth upon the throne, and unto the Lamb for ever and ever."— Declaratory Minute of the Yearly Meeting, 1829, occasioned by the doctrinal divisions taking place among American Friends, which made London Yearly Meeting desire to make its own position clear.*

Wherefore, beloved brethren, . . . let it be the frequent engagement of your souls, in deep reverence and humility, to " consider the Apostle and High Priest of our profession, Christ Jesus." The promised Messiah, He to whom all preceding dispensations had pointed, and in whom they were ended and fulfilled, He who was with God, and was God, the Word who hath declared to man Him that is invisible, even He was made flesh, and dwelt amongst men. Though He was rich, yet for our sakes He became poor ; veiling, in the form of a servant, the brightness of His glory, that, through Him, the kindness and love of God toward men might appear, in a manner every way suited to our wants and finite capacities. His righteous precepts were illustrated and confirmed by His own holy example. He went about doing good ; for us He endured sorrow, hunger, thirst, weariness, pain ; unutterable anguish of body and of soul even unto death ; and was " in all

* The application made of the Old Testament passages follows the mode of thought of the time.

points tempted like as we are, yet without sin." Thus humbling Himself that we might be exalted, He emphatically recognised the duties and the sufferings of humanity as among the means whereby, through the obedience of faith, we are to be disciplined for heaven; sanctifying them to us, by Himself performing and enduring them; and, as "the Forerunner," at once plainly marking and consecrating for His followers the path in which they must tread. But not only in these blessed relations must the Lord Jesus be ever precious to His people. Exalted to be a Prince and a Saviour, in Him has been revealed a Redeemer at once able to suffer and almighty to save; an High Priest, "touched with the feeling of our infirmities," who, having made reconciliation for our sins by the offering up of Himself once for all, "is gone into heaven," there to appear, our Mediator and Advocate, in the presence of God.—From the *Yearly Meeting Epistle*, 1852.

"The Lord our God is holy"; and "His mercy endureth for ever." These great truths were proclaimed under the old covenant. But it is in the glorious Gospel that their harmony is clearly unfolded, and the way revealed whereby fallen man may be made a partaker, through faith, of the righteousness of God. . . .

The Gospel is a message of glad tidings to man as he is, in order that he may become what he is not. It deals, not with speculation, but with fact. . . . "All have sinned and come short of the glory of God." . . . Sin is indeed a fearful reality. It is in its essence a revolt against God. The Gospel is the recognition of the disease, and God's offer to all of the one remedy. "The wrath of God," of which we are so often impressively reminded in the New as well as in the Old Testament, is, in the light of the Gospel, the active manifestation of His holiness altogether free from any approach to earthly passion or vindictiveness. The Father's heart still yearns over the lost child. . . . "God commendeth His love toward us, in that, while we were yet sinners, Christ died for us."—From the *Yearly Meeting Epistles*, 1868, 1881.

The Offering Up of Christ

The offering of our Lord Jesus Christ as the sacrifice for sin is the manifestation of the holiness and love of God, in which He, the unchangeably Just, proclaims Himself " the justifier of him that believeth in Jesus." . . . From age to age the sufferings and death of Christ have been a hidden mystery and a rock of offence to the unbelief and pride of man's fallen nature ; yet to the humble penitent, whose heart is broken under the convicting power of the Spirit, life is revealed in that death. As he looks upon Him who was wounded for our transgressions, and upon whom the Lord was pleased to lay the iniquity of us all, his eye is more and more opened to see, and his heart to understand, the awfulness of sin, for which the Saviour died ; whilst, in the sense of pardoning grace, he may " joy in God, through our Lord Jesus Christ, by whom we have now received the atonement."—From the *Yearly Meeting Epistle*, 1868.

The Cross of Christ

Now that ye know the power of God and are come to it— which is the Cross of Christ, that crucifies you to the state that Adam and Eve were in in the fall, and so [crucifies you] to the world—by this power of God ye come to see the state they were in before they fell, which power of God is the Cross, in which stands the everlasting glory ; which brings up into the righteousness, holiness and image of God, and crucifies to the unrighteousness, unholiness and image of Satan.—George Fox, 1624-1691, Epistle written in 1656, in *Journal*, Bi-centenary edition, 1891, vol. I, p. 345.

"I and the Father are one." That means to me that I think of God in terms of Jesus Christ, that I pray to Jesus as representing the Father to my consciousness, or to the Father as I see Him in Jesus. Carry that thought to Calvary itself. See in the Crucifixion not merely a martyr's death, not merely a passing gleam of God's love, certainly not a sacrifice to God carrying a legal significance, but in truth the flashing into light of an eternal fact, the nature of God's relation to sin, of the pain we inflict on His heart by our own wrong-doing. Here is the wonderful dynamic of the Cross. God calls you to Him. He shows you His suffering, He shows you the hatefulness of the sin that caused it, and, in showing you His love, shows you the punishment of alienation from Him, the hell of the unrepentant, in which we must remain until repentance opens the gate for the prodigal and gives entrance to the free forgiveness and love of the Father's house. In Jesus, in His life and His death upon the cross, we are shown the nature of God, and the possibilities that are within our reach. We are shown the world as the Father sees it, are called to live in harmony with His will and purpose, to hate the sins that made Him mourn, to scale the barrier of sin and discover that the way of penitence lies open and direct to the Fatherly heart. No legal bargain, but a spiritual conflict, an inward change, the rejection of the living death of sin, the choice of the new birth, of the purified self, the conversion from a low and earthly to a high and spiritual standard of life and conduct—here you have the practical conditions of salvation, and, in the active, free and holy love of God, ever seeking entrance, ever powerful if we but yield the gateway of our heart, is the substance of the Gospel. The revelation of God's Fatherhood, and the possi-bility of unity with Him through Christ, meet the deep need of the soul for a centre of repose apart from the transitory interests and the things of time. Hear then the gentle appeal, " Come unto Me and rest."—John Wilhelm Rowntree, 1868-1905, *Essays and Addresses*, 1906, pp. 361, 362.

The radiant vision of Christ, who reveals to us the Father, will be our inspiration for service. As we know more of the meaning of His life and of His death we shall learn the secret of His conquering love. His cross will be to us

" No fable old, nor mythic lore,
    Nor dream of bards and seers,
  No dead fact stranded on the shore
      Of the oblivious years,"

nor will it be a doctrine without compelling power over our hearts' affections. It will be a manifestation at once of the Divine holiness that condemns sin and of the love that forgives and restores. It is in the victory of the Cross that we too shall conquer; as we join with the apostle in being crucified with Christ, we shall know that He lives in us. His conquest of death is the pledge that as we are willing to die to self we too shall live: "the power of His resurrection" is closely linked with "the fellowship of His sufferings." In the strength of that victory we can take our place with cheerful and trustful hearts in the great conflict which throughout human history has been waged between the powers of good and evil. We go forth conquering and to conquer through Him who loves us. —From the *Yearly Meeting Epistle*, 1909.

Preaching Jesus

The Lord Jesus Christ and His redeeming love must be the central theme of all our preaching, for only thus can the deepest needs of men's hearts be met. It is still true that the Cross of Christ is to some a "stumbling-block," and to some "foolishness." Yet it is our firm conviction that in the right appreciation and appropriation of the atoning work of our Lord Jesus Christ there lies the secret of a successful life. Let us proclaim this with holy confidence, taking care at the same time that our message is a living truth to our own souls, and not one to which we give a mere intellectual assent.—From the *Yearly Meeting Epistle*, 1904.

Jesus and the Children

We turn with loving interest to the children and young people of our religious Society. To you, dear children, we send a special message. We want you to think of the love of Jesus; how for you He became a little child, how He gave Himself for you when He died upon the Cross; and how He asks you to let Him come by His spirit into your hearts that He may be your own loving Saviour and Friend. The children of

Jerusalem once welcomed Him to the temple with words of
gladness ; will you not welcome Him now into your hearts ?
Your life is like a boat upon the sea ; you cannot guide it safely
yourselves, for you know not the dangers and difficulties that
may be in your course.   Jesus knows them all ; and, if you ask
Him, He will come into your little boat to guide it safely all the
way.   How happy are the children who have Him with them
every hour.   We are glad to know that many of you have this
joy.   We want you all to have it.—From the *Yearly Meeting
Epistle*, 1895.

Our Lord and Master

In joy of inward peace, or sense
  Of sorrow over sin,
He is His own best evidence,
  His witness is within.

No fable old, nor mythic lore,
  Nor dream of bards and seers,
No dead fact stranded on the shore
  Of the oblivious years,

But warm, sweet, tender, even yet
  A present help is He :
And faith has still its Olivet,
  And love its Galilee.

The healing of His seamless dress
  Is by our beds of pain ;
We touch Him in life's throng and press,
  And we are whole again.

Through Him the first fond prayers are said
  Our lips of childhood frame,
The last low whispers of our dead
  Are burdened with His name.

Our Lord and Master of us all !
   Whate'er our name or sign,
We own Thy sway, we hear Thy call,
   We test our lives by Thine.

     .   .   .   .

We faintly hear, we dimly see,
   In differing phrase we pray ;
But, dim or clear, we own in Thee
   The Light, the Truth, the Way !

     .   .   .   .

—From *Our Master*, by J. G. Whittier, 1807-1892.

CHAPTER VII

THE SCRIPTURES

And as concerning the Holy Scriptures, we do believe that they were given forth by the Holy Spirit of God, through the holy men of God, who, as the Scripture itself declares (2 Pet. i. 21), " spake as they were moved by the Holy Ghost." We believe they are to be read, believed and fulfilled—He that fulfils them is Christ—and they are " profitable for doctrine, for reproof, for correction and for instruction in righteousness, that the man of God may be perfect, throughly furnished unto all good works " (2 Tim. iii. 16, 17), and are able to make wise " unto salvation through faith in Christ Jesus." . . . We call the Holy Scriptures, as Christ and the Apostles called them, and holy men of God called them, *viz.*: the " words of God.'' . . . We do declare that we do esteem it a duty incumbent on us to pray with and for, to teach, instruct and admonish those in and belonging to our families.—Epistle addressed by George Fox and others to the Governor of Barbadoes, in 1671, *Journal,* 1694 edition, pp. 359, 360. Bi-centenary edition, 1891, vol. II, pp. 156-158.

George Fox says (1656), in an Answer for clearing Truth and Friends from slanders, &c. (*Journal,* Bi-centenary edition, i. 306):—"And do not the ministers of God say, that the Scriptures are a declaration which you call the Word ? Do you not rob Christ of His title and of His honour and give it to the letter, and show yourselves out of the doctrine of the ministers of God, who call the Scriptures by the name of writings and treatises and declarations ; and who said, Christ's name is called the Word of God ? "

From these revelations of the Spirit of God to the saints have proceeded the Scriptures of Truth, which contain :—

(1) A faithful historical account of the actions of God's people in divers ages, with many singular and remarkable providences attending them.

(2) A prophetical account of several things, whereof some are already past, and some are yet to come.

(3) A full and ample account of all the chief principles of the doctrine of Christ, held forth in divers precious declarations, exhortations and sentences, which, by the moving of God's Spirit, were at several times and upon sundry occasions spoken and written unto some Churches and their pastors.

Nevertheless, because they are only a declaration of the fountain and not the fountain itself, therefore they are not to be esteemed the principal ground of all truth and knowledge, nor yet the adequate, primary rule of faith and manners. Yet, because they give a true and faithful testimony of the first foundation, they are and may be esteemed a secondary rule, subordinate to the Spirit, from which they have all their excellency and certainty : for, as by the inward testimony of the Spirit we do alone truly know them, so they testify that the Spirit is that Guide by which the saints are led into all truth : therefore, according to the Scriptures the Spirit is the first and principal Leader.—Robert Barclay, 1648-1690, *Apology*, Proposition III.

We have shown what service and use the Holy Scriptures, as managed in and by the Spirit, are of to the Church of God, wherefore we do account them a secondary rule. Moreover, because they are commonly acknowledged by all to have been written by the dictates of the Holy Spirit, and that the errors which may be supposed by the injury of time to have slipped in are not such but that there is a sufficient clear testimony left to all the essentials of the Christian faith, we do look upon them as the only fit outward judge of controversies among Christians, and that whatsoever doctrine is contrary unto their testimony may therefore justly be rejected as false.—*Ibid.*, Proposition III, sect. 6.

We can truly say concerning the Scriptures, that now we believe, not so much because of the relation of things concerning Christ which we have found in them, but because we have seen and received the thing which the Scriptures speak of.—Isaac Penington, 1616-1679, *A Question to the Professors of Christianity*, 1667, in *Works*, 1681 edition, Part II, p. 6.

Often as our religious Society has declared its belief in the divine authority of the Holy Scriptures, and upheld the sacred volume as the only divinely authorised record of the doctrines of true religion, we believe it right at this time to revive some important declarations of Scripture itself on the subject. It is expressly declared by the apostle Peter, that "the prophecy came not in old time by the will of man : but holy men of God spake as they were moved by the Holy Ghost." The apostle John declares respecting the gospel which he wrote, "These are written, that ye might believe that Jesus is the Christ, the Son of God ; and that believing ye might have life through his name." Very pertinent and comprehensive is the language which the apostle Paul addressed to Timothy : "From a child thou hast known the Holy Scriptures, which are able to make thee wise unto salvation through faith which is in Christ Jesus. All Scripture is given by inspiration of God, and is profitable for doctrine, for reproof, for correction, for instruction in righteousness : that the man of God may be perfect, throughly furnished unto all good works." Again, the apostle says, "Whatsoever things were written aforetime were written for our learning, that we through patience and comfort of the Scriptures might have hope." Finally, our blessed Lord, in reference to those divine writings of which the grand object in accordance with His own declaration, was to testify of Himself, emphatically declares "The Scripture cannot be broken."—From the *Yearly Meeting Epistle*, 1836.

People say that the Bible is like a chain, and that no chain can be stronger than its weakest link ; but the Bible is not like a chain. It is a library, for the word Bible comes from a word meaning not book but books, one volume may be of more importance than another without destroying the value of the rest.

The Bible does indeed now have to be regarded from an altered point of view. We cannot look upon it as an infallible teacher on points of history, or geology, or astronomy, for it is not. We cannot be sure as to the authorship of certain parts that we used to think unquestioned. But it remains true that it contains a record of God's dealings with men, and that here we have, under the illumination of the same spirit as was in the people who wrote, the needed teaching and safe guidance. —Richard H. Thomas, of Baltimore, *Life and Letters*, by Anna B. Thomas, 1905, pp. 388, 389.

We believe in the inspiration of the Bible, as the record of a progressive self-revelation of God to men, in proportion as their eyes were open to receive it; a revelation gradually unfolded to men in the spiritual experience of prophets and psalmists, and culminating in the perfect manifestation given in Jesus Christ. We do not call the Scriptures " the Word of God ", holding that this phrase has a larger and more inclusive meaning, as it has undoubtedly in John i. 1-14. We believe that it was because the Spirit of Jesus revealed the truth to His followers that they were able to receive Him and to appreciate His redemptive work; and that it is only as the same Spirit enlightens our own hearts that we can use the Scriptures aright. The Spirit that inspired prophets and apostles of old still breathes in the souls of men, and is ever leading all childlike spirits to a deeper knowledge of the hidden things of God.—Statement prepared by a Committee of London and Middlesex Quarterly Meeting, 1918, and printed in the *Yearly Meeting Proceedings*, 1919.

The Canon of Scripture may be closed, but the inspiration of the Holy Spirit has not ceased. We believe that there is no literature in the world where the revelation of God is given so fully as in our New Testament Scriptures; we go back to them for light and life and truth. But we feel that the life comes to us, not from the record itself, but from communion with Him of whom the record tells. Through His own Spirit we commune with Him Himself. In the words of Coleridge :—" I meet that in Scripture which finds me." . . . We feel them to be inspired, because they inspire us ; we go to them for guidance because as we read them we feel our eyes are being opened and our spirits kindled. . . . We search them because " these are they that testify of *Me*." It is the living Christ we want to find, the eternal revealer of the will of God. It is the spirit behind the letter that we need.—Statement prepared by York- shire Quarterly Meeting, 1919, and printed in the *Yearly Meeting Proceedings*, 1919.

See also *Christian Practice*, chap. i, sect. vi, "The Reading and Study of the Bible."

Chapter VIII

THE CHURCH

The Church is to be considered as it signifies a certain number of persons gathered by God's Spirit . . . unto the belief of the true principles and doctrines of the Christian Faith, who, through their hearts being united by the same love and their understandings informed in the same truths, gather, meet and assemble together to wait upon God, to worship Him and to bear a joint testimony for the truth against error, suffering for the same. And so becoming, through this fellowship, as one family and household in certain respects, [they] do each of them watch over, teach, instruct and care for one another, according to their several measures and attainments.—Robert Barclay, 1648-1690, *Apology*, Proposition X, sect. 3.

It is the life of Christianity taking place in the heart that makes a Christian ; and so it is a number of such being alive, joined together in the life of Christianity, that make a Church of Christ ; and it is all those that are thus alive and quickened, considered together, that make the catholic Church of Christ. Therefore, when this life ceaseth in one, then that one ceaseth to be a Christian ; and all power, virtue and authority which he had as a Christian ceaseth with it. . . . And as it is of one, so of many, yea, of a whole Church ; for seeing nothing makes a man truly a Christian but the life of Christianity inwardly ruling in his heart, so nothing makes a Church but the gathering of several true Christians into one body.—*Ibid.*, Proposition X, sect. 10.

The Power of God

The Power of God is the authority of the men's and women's meetings and of all the other meetings. All the faithful men and women, in every city, county and nation, whose faith stands in the Power of God, the Gospel of Christ, and have received this gospel and are in possession of this gospel, the Power of God, they have all right to the power of the meetings, for they be heirs of the power and the authority of the men's and women's meetings.—*Epistle from the Yearly Meeting of Ministers,* 1676.

Unity and Concord

Being orderly come together [you are] not to spend time with needless, unnecessary and fruitless discourses, but to proceed in the wisdom of God . . . not in the way of the world, as a worldly assembly of men, by hot contests, by seeking to outspeak and overreach one another in discourse, as if it were controversy between party and party of men, or two sides violently striving for dominion . . . not deciding affairs by the greater vote . . . but in the wisdom, love and fellowship of God, in gravity, patience, meekness, in unity and concord, submitting one to another in lowliness of heart, and in the holy Spirit of Truth and righteousness, all things [are] to be carried on ; by hearing, and determining every matter coming before you in love, coolness, gentleness and dear unity ;—I say, as one only party, all for the truth of Christ and for the carrying on the work of the Lord, and assisting one another in whatsoever ability God hath given ; and to determine of things by a general mutual concord, in assenting together as one man in the spirit of truth and equity, and by the authority thereof. In this way and spirit all things are to be amongst you, and without perverseness, in any self-separation, in discord and partiality ; this way and spirit is wholly excepted, as not worthy to enter into the assembly of God's servants . . . in any case pertaining to the service of the Church of Christ, in which His Spirit of love and unity must rule.— Testimony, 1662, of Edward Burrough, 1633-1663, *Letters of Early Friends,* 1841, p. 305.

Membership*

The least member in the Church hath an office and is service-able, and every member hath need one of another.—George Fox, *Epistles*, 1698 edition, p. 290.

It is they only who are washed, who are sanctified, who are justified, in the name of the Lord Jesus, and by the Spirit of our God, who can enjoy the unspeakable privilege of membership in [the Lord's] spiritual Israel.   No rite, no outward membership in any church, can suffice to make us children of Abraham. . . . Without conversion they who have but a birthright amongst us may, notwithstanding all their advantages of training and education, grow old, still inquiring, like Nicodemus, " How can these things be ? "   To every member of each successive generation the answer of the Lord is alike applicable, " Ye must be born again."   Without this essential change none can see the kingdom of God.   Let none, therefore, allow themselves to be deceived. . . . The words of our Lord and Master cannot be reversed, " Except ye be converted and become as little children, ye shall not enter into the kingdom of heaven."—From the *Yearly Meeting Epistles*, 1854, 1881.

Worship of God

The Worship of God under the Gospel consists not in ceremonies or in external observances.   It is a simple *spiritual* service.   That which was represented in the sacrifices of the law was fulfilled and ended in the Lord Jesus Christ, and in the exercise of faith in Him, the reality is now to be enjoyed.   " He is the propitiation for our sins," the High Priest who hath passed into the heavens, now to appear our Mediator and Advocate, in the presence of God.   We cannot doubt that the outward observances ordained under the former dispensation were blessed to the children of God through faith ; but even

* See also *Church Government*, chap. III.

8

then the testimony of the Spirit, from generation to generation, pointed with ever increasing clearness to the eternal Substance ; even then, one prophet after another was called to proclaim the truth embodied in the words, " Thou desirest not sacrifice, else would I give it ; Thou delightest not in burnt offering. The sacrifices of God are a broken spirit ; a broken and a contrite heart, O God, Thou wilt not despise." . . .

No worship ought now to be made dependent upon the presence of any one man or order of men ; no service, or stated vocal utterance in the congregation, ought to be allowed to interfere with the operations of the Lord's free Spirit. We thankfully recognise, as a means of edification, the preaching of the Gospel, and offerings of public prayer or thanksgiving, under the renewed anointing of the Holy Ghost ; but we dare not make these dependent upon human arrangements, or exclude, by any such arrangements, the unseen, but not unfelt ministrations of the Spirit of Christ, " dividing to every man severally, as He wills."—From the *Yearly Meeting Epistle*, 1866.

The Authority of Christ in His Church

It is the prerogative of Christ to call and qualify by the Holy Spirit His servants to minister in word and doctrine, and to preach repentance towards God, and faith towards our Lord Jesus Christ. In the earliest period of the Christian Church His Spirit was, agreeably to ancient prophecy, poured upon servants and upon handmaidens ; and we believe He continues to call, from the young and from the old, from the unlearned and from the wise, from the poor and from the rich, from women as well as from men, those whom He commissions to declare unto others the way of salvation. . . .

The servants of Christ who labour in the ministry are to be highly esteemed for their work's sake ; and when they leave their outward avocations, at His call, to preach the Gospel, their outward wants should be cheerfully supplied, if needful. Yet we consider the gift of the ministry to be of so pure and sacred a nature, that no payment should be made for its exercise, and that it ought never to be undertaken for pecuniary remuneration. As the gift is free, the exercise of it ought to be free also, in accordance with the precept of our Lord, " Freely ye have received, freely give."—From an Address issued by the Yearly Meeting, 1841.

Spiritual Priesthood

The earthly pilgrimage of the Christian is not to be a solitary one ; he has become a member of a body, a citizen of a heavenly Kingdom, a constituent part of the household of faith. The followers of Christ are, in the words of the Apostle Peter, to be " built up a spiritual house, a holy priesthood, to offer up spiritual sacrifices, acceptable to God through Jesus Christ " (1 Pet. ii. 5). It was to the whole company of Christians in Asia Minor, not to any special order, that these words were addressed ; it was the whole company of Christians at Rome whom the Apostle besought " by the mercies of God " (Rom. xii. 1) to render a holy, acceptable and reasonable service, through the dedication of their bodies " a living sacrifice " unto God. For the redeemed man, the incarnation of Christ has consecrated all life ; to him the distinction between things secular and things religious fades away ; whether he eats or drinks or whatsoever he does (1 Cor. x. 31), he recognises the glory of God to be his constant aim and object. Membership in the royal priesthood is not conditioned by the distinctions of age or sex. Especially, though by no means exclusively, in the ministries of home life are Christian women called to fulfil their spiritual priesthood, and we desire earnestly to urge them not to be neglectful of this holy calling. And how great is the privilege to themselves and to the Church when through obedience to the teachings of the Spirit of Truth, children are early introduced into the same honourable vocation. . . .
—From the *Yearly Meeting Epistle*, 1899.

CHAPTER IX

THE WAY OF LIFE

Religion is not a matter of form, but of the very life.—Robert Spence Watson, address at the Manchester Conference, 1895.

The Gospel religion is very precious, being inwardly felt and experienced in the life and power of it ; but a bare profession of it, out of the life and power of godliness, is of no value in the sight of God, nor is it of any profit or advantage to the soul.— Isaac Penington, *Works*, 1681 edition, Part II, p. 496.

The end of words (even of Christ's own directions in the days of His flesh) is to turn men to the holy life and power from whence the words came.—*Ibid*, p. 170.

It has ever been our belief that the light of Christ, the brightness of the Father's glory, is (through obedience to light, even while in ignorance of its Source) purifying the hearts of many who name not His Name—who are not yet able to recognise the Blessed Face from which the light shines. But the fullness of " the light which no man can approach unto " is surely reserved for those who stand before the throne of God and of the Lamb, and with full purpose of heart bow in adoration before Him that sitteth thereon.

We claim to be a people who have found rest in God ; a people building our house upon the rock, through obedience to those " words of eternal life " given forth by Christ, the Word. We recognise His Voice as speaking to us, not only in the pages of Scripture, but also in the whole course of life as ordered by Him ; and yet more closely in the inmost chamber of our own hearts ; and we desire to yield to it an undivided allegiance. —Caroline E. Stephen, *Quaker Strongholds*, 4th edition, 1907, p. 160.

The doctrine of the indwelling Spirit has been to the Friends neither a philosophical ideal, nor a pious opinion only, but an eminently practical faith, embracing within its scope the whole of human life. The presence of the Spirit gives the power to translate the Apostle's advice into practice, " Whether therefore ye eat, or drink, or whatsoever ye do, do all to the glory of God." Hence little account is made of the popular distinction between things secular and things religious ; all work, all times, every employment that is not wrong may be accounted holy. Conduct beyond the reach of human law is not outside the Divine law.—John S. Rowntree, *The Society of Friends : Its Faith and Practice*, 1919 edition, pp. 33, 34.

" Behold," says Christ Himself, " I stand at the door and knock ; if any man hear my voice and open the door, I will come in to him and sup with him and he with me " (Rev. iii. 20). What door can this be but that of the heart of man ?

Thou, like the inn of old, hast been full of other guests ; thy affections have entertained other lovers ; there has been no room for thy Saviour in thy soul. Wherefore salvation is not yet come into thy house, though it is come to thy door, and thou hast been often proffered it and hast profest it long. But if He calls, if He knocks still, that is, if His light yet shines, if it reproves thee still, there is hopes thy day is not over, and that repentance is not yet hid from thine eyes ; but His love is after thee still, and His holy invitation continues to save thee. . . .

So I say to thee, unless thou believest that He that stands at the door of thy heart and knocks, and sets thy sins in order before thee, and calls thee to repentance, be the Saviour of the world, thou wilt die in thy sins, and where His is gone thou wilt never come. For if thou believest not in Him, it is impossible that He should do thee good, or effect thy salvation ; Christ works not against faith, but by it. 'Tis said of old, He did not many mighty works in some places, because the people believed not in Him (Mark vi. 5). So that if thou truly believest in Him, thine ear will be attentive to His voice in thee, and the door of thine heart open to His knocks. Thou wilt yield to the discoveries of His light, and the teachings of His grace will be very dear to thee.

It is the nature of true faith to beget an holy fear of offending God, a deep reverence to His precepts, and a most tender regard to the inward testimony of His Spirit, as that by which His children in all ages have been safely led to glory. For, as they that truly believe, receive Christ in all His tenders to the soul, so as true it is that those who receive Him thus, with Him receive power to become the sons of God; that is an inward force and ability to do whatever He requires; strength to mortify their lusts, control their affections, resist evil motions, deny themselves, and overcome the world in its most enticing appearances. This is the life of the blessed Cross of Christ, which is the subject of the following discourse, and what thou, O man, must take up, if thou intendest to be the disciple of Jesus. Nor canst thou be said to receive Christ, or to believe in Him, whilst thou rejectest His Cross. For, as receiving of Christ is the means appointed of God to salvation, so bearing thy daily cross after Him, is the only true testimony of receiving Him, and therefore it is enjoined by Him as the great token of discipleship. "Whosoever will be my disciple, let him take up his daily cross and follow Me" (Matt. xvi. 24). . . .

Nor is a recluse life, the boasted righteousness of some, much more commendable, or one whit nearer to the nature of the true Cross; for if it be not unlawful as other things are, 'tis unnatural, which true religion teaches not. The Christian convent* and monastery are within, where the soul is encloistered from sin. . . .

The Cross of Christ is of another nature; it truly overcomes the world, and leads a life of purity in the face of its allurements; they that bear it are not thus chained up, for fear they should bite; nor locked up, lest they should be stole away; no, they receive power from Christ their Captain, to resist the evil, and do that which is good in the sight of God; to despise the world, and love its reproach above its praise; and not only not to offend others, but love those that offend them. . . . True

* "Convert" in the original.

godliness don't turn men out of the world, but enables them to live better in it, and excites their endeavours to mend it ; not hide their candle under a bushel, but set it upon a table in a candlestick. . . .

Taking up the Cross of Jesus is a more interior exercise ; it is the circumspection and discipline of the soul in conformity to the divine mind therein revealed. Does not the body follow the soul, and not the soul the body ? Do not such consider, that no outward cell can shut up the soul from lust, the mind from an infinity of unrighteous imaginations ? The thoughts of man's heart are evil, and that continually. Evil comes from within, and not from without ; how then can an external application remove an internal cause ? . . .

Whoever they are that would come to Christ, and be right Christians, must readily abandon every delight that would steal away the affections of the mind, and exercise it from the divine principle of life, and freely write a bill of divorce for every beloved vanity ; and all, under the Sun of Righteousness, is so, compared with Him.—William Penn, Second (1682) edition of *No Cross, No Crown,* from *Works,* 1726 edition, Vol. I, pp. 279, 280, 295, 296, 360.

It would go a great way to caution and direct people in their use of the world, that they were better studied and known in the creation of it. For how could men find the confidence to abuse it, while they should see the great Creator stare them in the face, in all and every part thereof ? Their ignorance makes them insensible ; and that insensibility hardy in misusing this noble creation, that has the stamp and voice of a Deity everywhere, and in everything, to the observing. It is too frequent to begin with God and end with the world. But He is the good man's beginning and end, his Alpha and Omega.

The humble, meek, merciful, just, pious and devout souls are everywhere of one religion ; and when death has taken off the mask, they will know one another though the divers liveries they wear here makes them strangers.

This world is a form ; our bodies are forms ; and no visible acts of devotion can be without forms. But yet the less form in religion the better, since God is a Spirit ; for the more mental our worship, the more adequate to the nature of God ; the more silent, the more suitable to the language of a Spirit.

Words are for others, not for ourselves ; nor for God, who hears not as bodies do, but as spirits should.

If we would know this dialect, we must learn of the divine principle in us. As we hear the dictates of that, so God hears us ; there we may see Him too in all His attributes ; though but in little, yet as much as we can apprehend or bear ; for as He is in Himself, He is incomprehensible, and " dwelleth in that light which no eye can approach." But in His image we may behold His glory ; enough to exalt our apprehensions of God ; and to instruct us in that worship which pleaseth Him.—Penn, *Some Fruits of Solitude*, 1718 edition, Nos. 12-14, 27, 519, 507-510.

Love silence even in the mind ; for thoughts are to that, as words to the body, troublesome ; much speaking, as much thinking, spends, and in many thoughts, as well as words, there is sin. True silence is the rest of the mind, and is to the spirit what sleep is to the body, nourishment and refreshment. It is a great virtue ; it covers folly, keeps secrets, avoids disputes, and prevents sin.—Penn, *Fruits of a Father's Love*, 1765 edition, pp. 23-24.

How little could those of whom we read in the Gospels suppose that the Jesus of Nazareth, who moved amongst them, was organising a vast Ecclesia. Nor is that our task. He who, on however small a scale, would imitate the Master in bringing in the Kingdom of Heaven, will find his life filled with humbler and simpler duties. Walk with men in the garden or in the grove. Meditate in the desert, and return to feed the hungry. Talk with the reaper in the field, or with the woman at the wayside well. Join the tramp on the road, or discuss with the learned in their long robes. Gather with your friends in an upper room to break bread in the evening. If you are filled with the spirit of the Master, all these little acts of human converse are contributions towards the building up of the

Church of Christ. You may not thus reconstruct a theology; you may be doing something far more vital for religion, pure and undefiled. For in the economy of Christ's teaching the vision of God is not reserved for the accomplished theologian ; it is accorded to the pure in heart.—Silvanus Phillips Thompson, 1851-1916, *A Not Impossible Religion,* 1918, pp. 39, 40.

As there is no true prostration of heart before Him without submission, no one can worship, in the true sense of the word, whose intentions and plans are consciously out of line with the Lord's will. If God is everywhere, and equally near to us at all times, and if the essence of spiritual worship consists in our inward attitude before Him, then nothing—however it may stimulate worship in its outward form—is worship apart from this inward condition of soul. There is no form or ceremony that can by itself be an act of worship ; neither can there be such a thing as worship by proxy.—Richard H. Thomas, *The Objects of Public Worship,* Yorkshire 1905 Committee Leaflet.

The Spirit of Christ, dealing with men as men, applying Himself to the ever-varying circumstances of time and place, is opposed to all artificial or ritual arrangements that divide us from men. The only separation from the world that Christ enjoins is that which has its root in a changed character. Our bodies are the temple of the Holy Ghost, and all who know this experimentally have true spiritual unity with all others who are in Christ. But outward ritual has far more effect in hiding this unity, and in separating the children of God than in uniting them. We therefore discard these outward rites, for membership in the true Christian Church has to do with character and is an inward experience. " He is not a Jew who is one outwardly." True baptism, like circumcision, is not of the letter, but of the spirit, " for the letter killeth, but the spirit giveth life."—Richard H. Thomas, *Baptism,* 1911, p. 9.

Without the introduction into our worship of the " consecrated elements," we do often in our religious meetings feel that we are . . . fed by an unseen hand. . . . Many of us at such times have, though in no carnal, material sense, been permitted to feel the real presence of Christ.—Thomas Hodgkin, *Our Churches*, 1898, p. 193.

A dedicated life is itself the great sacrament. . . .

Friends' attitude towards ceremonial rites is not a merely negative one. They affirm that the baptism of the Holy Ghost must be known by the Christian, and that the life of the redeemed soul must be constantly nourished by a spiritual feeding on Christ. They repudiate the frequent assertion that they " have no communicants "—all their people are, in theory, communicants. They are at one with the early Church in holding that many of the usages of human life, and many of the material substances around us, may be vehicles through which the spiritual life is nourished. As the sacramentum was in the first instance the soldier's oath, whereby he attested his loyalty to the Roman Emperor, and as the early Christians applied the term to the religious use of water, oil, wine, milk, honey, salt, to feet washing, kissing, bathing, eating and drinking, so the Friends thankfully recognise that numberless occurrences will, to the humble and attentive disciple, become invaluable helps in confirming his loyalty to Christ : the marriage tie, a daily reminder of his relationship to the Bridegroom of souls, every meal a time for remembering the Lord's death. Stephen Grellet, a saintly evangelist, wrote : " I think I can reverently say that I very much doubt whether since the Lord by His grace brought me into the faith of His dear Son, I have ever broken bread or drunk wine, even in the ordinary course of life, without the remembrance of, and some devout feeling regarding the broken body and the blood-shedding of my dear Lord and Saviour."—John S. Rowntree, *The Society of Friends : Its Faith and Practice*, 1919 edition, pp. 52, 54.

And Christ said to the Church of Laodicea, " Behold, I stand at the door and knock, if any man will hear my voice and will open the door, I will come in to him and sup with him and he with me " ; and this was the supper that Christ

preached to John and to the Church, after He was ascended ;
for John had taken the supper of the elements of bread and
wine in the same night that Christ was betrayed, before Christ
was crucified, but now John writes to the Church and tells
them of another supper . . . which is a nearer and a more
inward supper than taking the elements of bread and wine in
remembrance of Christ's death, which Christ gave to His
disciples before He was crucified and said, " As often as ye eat
this bread and drink this cup, do it in remembrance of me, and
to show forth His death till He come " ; but after Christ was
risen and ascended, He saith, " Behold, I stand at the door and
knock, if any man will hear my voice and open the door," to
wit, of his heart, mind and soul (by joining to the light, grace
and truth of Jesus), " I will come in to him and sup with him
and he with me " ; and is not . . . this supper beyond, and
a further supper, than taking the elements of bread and wine
in remembrance of His death ?—George Fox, *Gospel Truth
Demonstrated*, 1706, p. 903.

We confess our continued conviction that all the ceremonies
of the Jewish law were fulfilled and finished by the death of
Christ, and that no shadows in the worship of God were
instituted by our Lord, or have any place in the Christian
dispensation.—From the *Yearly Meeting Epistle*, 1835.

The worship which He appointed is a worship for which He
provided no ritual. It may be without words, as well as with
them ; but, whether in silence or in utterance, it " must be in
spirit and in truth." He is Himself the propitiation and the
High Priest, the " one Mediator between God and men."
Through Him all believers have the same privilege of free
" access by one Spirit unto the Father." No man, or order
of men, can worship for the rest. No priests distinct from the
congregation were appointed by Christ ; the whole company of
believers, redeemed by His blood, being themselves called,
under the anointing of the Spirit, to be " an holy priesthood, to
offer up spiritual sacrifices, acceptable to God by Jesus Christ."

The word *priest* is never applied in the New Testament to the Christian minister as such.

We desire to accept every command of our Lord Jesus Christ, in what we believe to be its true evangelical import, as absolutely conclusive. For obedience to His commands, " Swear not at all," " Love your enemies," many of our Friends in earlier and in later times, on both sides of the Atlantic, have endured grievous sufferings, some even unto death. The question of outward ordinances, is with us, a question, not as to the authority of Christ, but as to His real meaning. Language more explicit can scarcely be imagined than that referred to in the Epistle to the Hebrews, in which the prophet Jeremiah was inspired to portray the distinguishing features of the New Covenant. Outward rites were among the special marks of the Old Covenant. The New Covenant was to be the opposite of this, " not according to the Old." The prophecy of Jeremiah is the only place in the ancient Scriptures in which the term " a New Covenant " occurs. And may we not believe that in pronouncing the words, " This is my blood of the New Covenant,"* our Lord Jesus Christ appropriated to Himself this great prophecy, and thereby proclaimed the Gospel to be a dispensation, not of type or symbol, but of spiritual reality ? He is the Lamb of God, the true Passover, whose " precious blood," offered upon the cross once for all, is no typical, but a real, all-availing atonement, never to be repeated. The law to be written on the heart under this " New Covenant " is, in like manner, no symbol, but a most real experience : " the law of the Spirit of life in Christ Jesus " making " free from the law of sin and death."

It continues to be our settled conviction that, in establishing this " New Covenant," the Lord Jesus Christ did not design that there should be any rite or outward observance of permanent obligation in His Church. His teaching, as in His parables, or in the command to wash one another's feet, was often in symbols; but it ought ever to be received in the light of His own emphatic

* " Testament " being translated " Covenant " in Heb. viii. 8, and elsewhere.

declaration, " The words that I speak unto you, they are spirit, and they are life." His baptism is the baptism with " the Holy Ghost and with fire." He is Himself " the bread of life." The eating of His body and the drinking of His blood is not an outward act. They truly partake of them who habitually rest upon the sufferings and death of their Lord as their only hope and in whom the indwelling Spirit gives of the fullness which is in Christ. It is this inward and spiritual partaking which is, as we believe, the true supper of the Lord. The new commandment, under this " New Covenant," is, according to His own teaching, that of love,—a love like His own,—" as I have loved you "; love grounded on the " peace " given by Him, and sustained and made fruitful by a continual participation in His life. His presence with His Church is not to be by symbol or representation, but in the real communication of His own Spirit. " I will pray the Father, and He shall give you another Comforter, that He may abide with you for ever." In the withdrawal of His bodily presence, this blessed Comforter remains to the Church the pledge of the power and continued care of its exalted King. He convinces of sin ; He testifies of Jesus ; He takes of the things of Christ, communicating to the believer and to the Church, in a gracious abiding manifestation, the real presence of the Lord. As the great Remembrancer, through whom the promises are fulfilled, He needs no ritual or priestly intervention in bringing to the experience of the true commemoration and communion. " Behold, I stand at the door and knock ; if any man hear my voice, and open the door, I will come in to him, and will sup with him, and he with me."

To abide in Christ the living Vine, to continue in His love, to live loose from the world, as those whom He has chosen and redeemed out of the world,—these were the injunctions of our adorable Redeemer as He went out to His last sufferings ; these are His commands of perpetual obligation to His Church : and it is in the fulfilling of them that His followers enjoy the true communion—the fruit of His intercession, " that they all may be one."—From the *Yearly Meeting Epistle*, 1880.

Jesus, when He took up the little children and said, " Of such is the Kingdom of Heaven," was speaking of Jewish children, who, according to the Jewish custom would not have been baptised, and the Quaker position is really summed up in the words " John indeed baptised with water, but ye shall be baptised with the Holy Spirit."

It is the inward change, the inward purification, the spiritual fact and not the outward symbol, that belongs in truth to the Kingdom of God. Neither in the refusal to baptise nor to take the supper do Friends set forth a negation. They assert, on the contrary, the positive truth that the religious life is the inward life of the spirit. But no place or time can limit its action, nor any symbol adequately express it, and that therefore of necessity no priest can claim to intervene between that inward life and its source of strength and power.

To the soul that feeds upon the bread of life the outward conventions of religion are no longer needful. Hid with Christ in God, there is for him small place for outward rites, for all experience is a holy baptism, a perpetual supper with the Lord, and all life a sacrifice, holy and acceptable unto God. This hidden life, this inward vision, this immediate and intimate union between the soul and God, this, as revealed in Jesus Christ, is the basis of the Quaker faith.—John Wilhelm Rowntree, *Essays and Addresses*, 1906, pp. 100, 92.

Service in Daily Life

It remains to speak of the Way of Service, as it concerns the conduct of our ordinary work and business. Nowhere is the practical working of our faith put to a severer test, yet nowhere is there a nobler and more fruitful witness to be borne. Business in its essence is no mere selfish struggle for the necessities and luxuries of life, but " a vast and complex movement of social service." However some may abuse its methods for private ends, its true function is not to rob the community but to serve it. But, in the fierce competition which is so marked a feature of the present day, it has become very difficult, some would say impossible for those engaged in business to be wholly faithful to Christ. Christianity is challenged in the shop and in the office.

We have been touched with keen sympathy for our friends, whether employers or employed, who find themselves in this strait. We cannot here deal fully with this question, but we are sure there is an answer to the challenge, and that the light which shines upon the Way of Life, and gives us the distinction of things inwardly, will guide us to the answer. We venture to say to our business friends : There must be no faltering in the pursuit of right ; if it is clearly a question between obedience to our Lord and the claims of business, these claims must give way. Be faithful to the light you have, and follow your conscience, in the spirit of love to our Master. If for the time being there is loss and pain, which you must even share with those who are dear to you, you will not be forsaken in the sacrifice you have made.

Christianity is tested, not only in the shop and in the office, but also in the home. In the standard of living adopted by the home-makers, in the portion of income devoted to comforts, recreations and luxuries, in willingness to be content with simplicity, the members of a household, both older and younger, may bear witness that there is a Way of Life that does not depend on the abundance of the things possessed.—From the *Yearly Meeting Epistle*, 1911.

Led by the Holy Spirit, we shall be enabled to show to those around us that the Christian faith is no mere theoretical belief, but a living realisation of the abiding presence of Christ. In all the details of daily life—not only in the meeting house, but in the schoolroom, the workshop, the office, or the council chamber—wherever in God's providence our duty calls us, we may know the joy of being guided by His counsel and may find a sanctuary in the midst of our busy occupations. Lives thus consecrated to His service are amongst the most convincing evidences of the truth of Christianity. Clear expositions of doctrine have their place and value ; but they are far less effective than the humble Christ-like walk of a child of God. Our testimony to the non-necessity of water-baptism and of partaking outwardly of the Lord's supper will avail little if we do not ourselves give evidence of a real baptism with the Holy Spirit and a personal enjoyment of the true communion. Our protest against ritual in worship will not draw men to join with us in waiting upon God, if it is not unmistakably clear to those who come to our meetings that we have the Lord's presence amongst us ; that we experimentally know the Headship of Christ in His Church and that we are worshipping the Father in spirit and in truth.—From the *Yearly Meeting Epistle*, 1894.

The Creator of the earth is the owner of it. He gave us being thereon, and our nature requires nourishment from the produce of it. He is kind and merciful to His creatures ; and while they live answerably to the design of their creation, they are so far entitled to convenient subsistence that we may not justly deprive them of it. By the agreements and contracts of our predecessors, and by our own doings, some enjoy a much greater share of this world than others ; and while those possessions are faithfully improved for the good of the whole, it agrees with equity ; but he who, with a view to self-exaltation, causeth some to labour immoderately, and with the profits arising therefrom employs others in the luxuries of life, acts contrary to the gracious designs of Him who is the owner of the earth ; nor can any possessions, either acquired or derived from ancestors, justify such conduct. Goodness remains to be goodness, and the direction of pure wisdom is obligatory on all reasonable creatures.

Though the poor occupy our estates by a bargain, to which they in their poor circumstances agree, and we may ask even less than a punctual fulfilling of their agreement, yet if our views are to lay up riches, or to live in conformity to customs which have not their foundation in the truth, and our demands are such as require from them greater toil or application to business than is consistent with pure love, we invade their rights as inhabitants of a world of which a good and gracious God is the proprietor, and under whom we are tenants.

Were all superfluities and the desire of outward greatness laid aside, and the right use of things universally attended to, such a number of people might be employed in things useful as that moderate labour with the blessing of Heaven would answer all good purposes, and a sufficient number would have time to attend to the proper affairs of civil society. . . .

Our gracious Creator cares and provides for all His creatures. His tender mercies are over all His works ; and so far as true love influences our minds, so far we become interested in His workmanship and feel a desire to make use of every opportunity to lessen the distresses of the afflicted and to increase the happiness of the creation. Here we have a prospect of one common interest, from which our own is inseparable, so that to turn all that we possess into the channel of universal love becomes the business of our lives. . . .

Divine love imposeth no rigorous or unreasonable commands, but graciously points out the spirit of brotherhood and the way to happiness, in attaining which it is necessary that we relinquish all that is selfish. . . .

The greater part of the necessaries of life are so far perishable that each generation hath occasion to labour for them ; and when we look towards a succeeding age with a mind influenced by universal love, instead of endeavouring to exempt some from those cares which necessarily relate to this life, and to give them power to oppress others, we desire that they may all be the Lord's children and live in that humility and order becoming His family. Our hearts, being thus opened and enlarged, will feel content with a state of things as foreign to luxury and grandeur as that which our Redeemer laid down as a pattern. . . .

For, as He lived in perfect plainness and simplicity, the greatest in His family cannot by virtue of his station claim a right to live in worldly grandeur without contradicting Him who said, " It is enough for the disciple to be as his Master." . . .

Can we remember that we are the disciples of the Prince of

Peace, and the example of humility and plainness which He set for us, without feeling an earnest desire to be disentangled from everything connected with selfish customs in food, in raiment, in houses, and in all things else ? . . .

Oppression in the extreme appears terrible ; but oppression in more refined appearances remains to be oppression, and when the smallest degree of it is cherished it grows stronger and more extensive.

To labour for a perfect redemption from this spirit of oppression is the great business of the whole family of Christ Jesus in this world.—From *A Word of Remembrance and Caution to the Rich*. Printed in John Woolman's *Journal*, New Century edition, pp. 264, etc.

He whose tender mercies are over all His works hath placed a principle in the human mind, which incites to exercise goodness towards every living creature ; and this being singly attended to, people become tender-hearted and sympathising ; but when frequently and totally rejected, the mind becomes shut up in a contrary disposition.—John Woolman's *Journal*, New Century edition, p. 43.

I believe where the love of God is verily perfected and the true spirit of government watchfully attended to, a tenderness towards all creatures made subject to us will be experienced, and a care felt in us that we do not lessen that sweetness of life in the animal creation which the Great Creator intends for them under our government.—John Woolman's *Journal*, New Century edition, p. 229.

Christian Service Abroad

Every one to the ministry, yourselves, which is the Seed, Christ ; for England is as a family of prophets, which must spread over all the nations ; as a garden of plants, and the place where the pearl is found which must enrich all nations with the heavenly treasure, out of which shall the waters of life flow and water all the thirsty ground ; and out of which nation and dominion must go the spiritually-weaponed and armed men to fight and conquer all nations, and bring them to the nation of God, that the Lord may be known to be the living God of nations, and His Son to reign, and His people [to be] one. —From the *Epistle from Skipton General Meeting, 25th of Second Month,* 1660.

Let all nations hear the sound by word or writing. Spare no place, spare no tongue nor pen, but be obedient to the Lord God ; go through the work and be valiant for the Truth upon earth ; tread and trample all that is contrary under. . . . Be patterns, be examples in all countries, places, islands, nations, wherever you come, that your carriage and life may preach among all sorts of people, and to them ; then you will come to walk cheerfully over the world, answering that of God in every one.—George Fox, To Friends in the Ministry, from Launceston prison, 1656, *Journal,* 1694 edition, pp. 212, 213. Bi-centenary edition, 1891, Vol. I, pp. 315, 316.

See also *Christian Practice*, chap. vi., sect. ii., " A World-wide Service."

Testimony for Peace

War, in our view, involves the surrender of the Christian ideal and a denial of human brotherhood ; it is an evil for the destruction of which the world is longing ; but freedom from the scourge of war will only be brought about through the faithfulness of individuals to their inmost convictions, under the guidance of the Spirit of Christ.

Our position is based upon our interpretation of the teaching of Jesus Christ.—Minute of *Adjourned Yearly Meeting, 1st Month,* 1916.

See also *Christian Practice*, chap. vii., sect. vii., " The International Kingdom."

In considering the character and basis of our testimony for Peace we have felt strongly that its deepest foundation lies in the nature of God, and that its character must be inclusive of the whole of life.

There is urgent need for a fuller recognition that God's essential nature is love, that the Cross of Jesus represents the highest point in the revelation of the character of God, and that there is a seed of God in every man, that spiritual forces are the mightiest, and that we must be prepared to rely upon them and to give expression to them in daily work and character as well as in what we call the great crises of life.

We must set before us the highest ideal, that which ought to be, rather than that which is, believing that God is not alone the God of things as they are but the God of things as they are meant to be !—Minute of *All Friends' Conference*, 1920.

The roots of war can be taken away from all our lives, as they were long ago in Francis of Assisi and John Woolman. Day by day let us seek out and remove every seed of hatred and of greed, of resentment and of grudging, in our own selves and in the social structure about us. Christ's way of freedom replaces slavish obedience by fellowship. Instead of an external compulsion He gives an inward authority. Instead of self-seeking, we must put sacrifice ; instead of domination, co-operation. Fear and suspicion must give place to trust and the spirit of understanding. Thus shall we more and more become friends to all men and our lives will be filled with the joy which true friendship never fails to bring. Surely this is the way in which Christ calls us to overcome the barriers of race and class and thus to make of all humanity a society of friends.—From *To Friends and Fellow Seekers,* Message of All Friends' Conference, 1920.

Foundations of a True Social Order

(1) The Fatherhood of God, as revealed by Jesus Christ, should lead us toward a Brotherhood which knows no restriction of race, sex or social class.

(2) This Brotherhood should express itself in a social order which is directed, beyond all material ends, to the growth of personality truly related to God and man.

(3) The opportunity of full development, physical, moral and spiritual, should be assured to every member of the community, man, woman and child. The development of man's full personality should not be hampered by unjust conditions nor crushed by economic pressure.

(4) We should seek for a way of living that will free us from the bondage of material things and mere conventions, that will raise no barrier between man and man, and will put no excessive burden of labour upon any by reason of our superfluous demands.

(5) The spiritual force of righteousness, loving-kindness and trust is mighty because of the appeal it makes to the best in every man, and when applied to industrial relations achieves great things.

(6) Our rejection of the methods of outward domination and of the appeal to force applies not only to international affairs, but to the whole problem of industrial control. Not through antagonism but through co-operation and goodwill can the best be attained for each and all.

(7) Mutual service should be the principle upon which life is organised. Service, not private gain, should be the motive of all work.

(8) The ownership of material things, such as land and capital, should be so regulated as best to minister to the need and development of man.—Accepted by the *Yearly Meeting*, 1918. *Printed Proceedings*, pp. 78, 80.

The Kingdom of Heaven on Earth

We have been led step by step to a profound realisation of a love which unites us in spiritual fellowship with seekers everywhere.

We have tried to face very frankly the facts of the world as it is, knowing that this must be our point of departure for the world as it ought to be. The war has aroused us to a sense of the moral failure of a civilisation which thwarts the practice of love in our social and international relationships. We have faith that out of the chaos of to-day will emerge a new order. This will be achieved as we individually strive to live so that the Divine Spirit is liberated in us.

Jesus has shown us how the sense of God as our common Father may permeate the whole of life. He has shown us that all final solutions of human problems are in terms of personal relationship and mutual understanding. We realise therefore, that we must strive to carry the pure spirit of love into all our dealings with men. The sacredness of personality demands a fundamental change in our social and economic system. This, however, does not absolve us from our immediate duty. We are called to live as citizens of the new world while still in the old. We recognise the difficulty of such a task, and that for its achievement our individual lives and corporate fellowship must be founded deep in unity with God. Quakerism for us means just that God-conscious life, and we desire to pass on to others the vision we have seen.

With the humility born of our failure to live out the principles that we profess, yet with the boldness of those who feel the greatness of their message, we would throw in our lives with all men and women who are sharing in the adventure of establishing the Kingdom of Heaven on Earth.—Minute of the *International Conference of Young Friends,* held at Jordans, 1920.

Walking with God

"Enoch walked with God." Is it not to such a walk that we also are called ? In this walk, the Christian is made a living evidence of the truth of his holy profession. Born of the Spirit, he is not his own. His desire is not so much to *speak* great things, as to *live* them. His whole life becomes a continued assertion of the power, presence and reign of his risen Redeemer, of whom he can say with the Apostle, He " loved me and gave Himself for me." It is his joy to know that in all his engagements, whether at home or abroad, in private or in public, on his farm, in his daily labour, in the pursuits of literature or of commerce, in the board-room or the council-chamber, his Lord

and Saviour is ever to reign supreme.   Is it not by a life such
as this that Christianity is to be commended to the masses
around us ?

Beloved Friends, is such a life ours ?   Let us never forget
that for its maintenance and growth, amidst the varied claims of
business and daily duty, the importance of waiting upon God in
private retirement and prayer cannot be over-estimated.   Without this our religious profession must be a fading flower.   The
lamp of the Christian's life cannot burn with brightness without
the continual supply of the heavenly oil.   It is his privilege to
know that even amidst the ceaseless pressure of his engagements,
he may live in communion with his God and Saviour.   How
many have found that in such a communion they are not only
afresh instructed in the lessons of their Saviour's love, but
receive a renewal of strength to go forth and to obey with
alacrity and joy.—From the *Yearly Meeting Epistle,* 1889.

The Way of Life

Early hath Life's mighty question
   Thrilled within thy heart of youth,
With a deep and strong beseeching :
   What and where is Truth ?

Hollow creed and ceremonial,
   Whence the ancient life hath fled,
Idle faith unknown to action,
   Dull and cold and dead.

Oracles, whose wire-worked meanings
   Only wake a quiet scorn,—
Not from these thy seeking spirit
   Hath its answer drawn.

   .   .   .   .

And to thee an answer cometh
   From the earth and from the sky,
And to thee the hills and waters
   And the stars reply.

But a soul-sufficing answer
　　Hath no outward origin ;
More than Nature's many voices
　　May be heard within.

　　　·　　·　　·　　·　　·

Not to ease and aimless quiet
　　Doth that inward answer tend,
But to works of love and duty
　　As our being's end ;

Not to idle dreams and trances,
　　Length of face, and solemn tone,
But to Faith, in daily striving
　　And performance shown.

Earnest toil and strong endeavour
　　Of a spirit which within
Wrestles with familiar evil
　　And besetting sin ;

And without, with tireless vigour,
　　Steady heart, and weapon strong,
In the power of truth assailing
　　Every form of wrong.

—From *To* ——, *with a copy of Woolman's Journal,*
　　　　　　　　　　　by J. G. Whittier.

Back to thyself is measured well
　　All thou hast given ;
Thy neighbour's wrong is thy present hell,
　　His bliss, thy heaven.

And in life, in death, in dark and light,
　　All are in God's care :
Sound the black abyss, pierce the deep of night,
　　And He is there !

　　　　—From *My Soul and I*, by J. G. Whittier.

Dear Lord and Father of mankind,
  Forgive our foolish ways !
Re-clothe us in our rightful mind,
In purer lives Thy service find,
  In deeper reverence, praise.

In simple trust like theirs who heard
  Beside the Syrian sea
The gracious calling of the Lord,
Let us, like them, without a word,
  Rise up, and follow Thee.

O Sabbath rest by Galilee !
  O calm of hills above.
Where Jesus knelt to share with Thee
The silence of eternity
  Interpreted by Love !

With that deep hush subduing all
  Our words and works that drown
The tender whisper of Thy call,
As noiseless let Thy blessing fall
  As fell Thy manna down.

Drop Thy still dews of quietness,
  Till all our strivings cease ;
Take from our souls the strain and stress
And let our ordered lives confess
  The beauty of Thy peace.

Breathe through the heats of our desire
  Thy coolness and Thy balm :
Let sense be dumb, let flesh retire ;
Speak through the earthquake, wind, and fire,
  O still, small voice of calm !

  —From *The Brewing of Soma*, by J. G. Whittier.

Believe and trust.   Through stars and suns,
　　Through life and death, through soul and sense,
His wise, paternal purpose runs ;
　　The darkness of His providence
　　Is star-lit with benign intents.

O joy supreme !   I know the Voice,
　　Like none beside on earth or sea ;
Yea, more, O soul of mine, rejoice,
　　By all that He requires of me,
　　I know what God Himself must be.

No picture to my aid I call,
　　I shape no image in my prayer ;
I only know in Him is all
　　Of life, light, beauty, everywhere,
　　Eternal Goodness here and there !

I know He is, and what He is,
　　Whose one great purpose is the good
Of all.   I rest my soul on His
　　Immortal Love and Fatherhood :
　　And trust Him, as His children should.

　　　　　　　—From *Revelation,* by J. G. Whittier.

　　See also *Christian Practice*, chap vii., sect. vi., " The Christian
Social Order."

Chapter X

RELIGIOUS PROBLEMS

Unsettlement of Faith

It may be true of some that when for the time they ought to be teachers, they have need that one teach them again which be the first principles of the oracles of God. In common with other Christian bodies, we have been no strangers to the unsettlement of faith which has accompanied recent movements of thought. The spirit of fearless inquiry has exercised itself within the borders of our own religious Society, yet we believe that behind these upheavals there has been a divine hand which has been removing the things that can be shaken, so that those things which cannot be shaken may remain. But, if this be the case, is it not also true that there has been and is a large amount of doubt which is the direct result of intellectual and spiritual indolence and feebleness ? Whatever may be the mental or spiritual process, the unsettlement of the faith of the individual means a lessening of the force of the appeal of the Church to the world.

At a time of personal unsettlement, Pascal wrote : " Seeing too much for denial and too little for assurance, I am in a piteous plight." . . . Those who may be thus exercised we greet in the spirit of hope as well as of earnest entreaty. We believe that as you are faithful to the convictions of the Holy Spirit, you will experience the blessedness of the prophetic words : " Thy sun shall no more go down ; neither shall thy moon withdraw itself ; for the Lord shall be thine everlasting light, and the days of thy mourning shall be ended."

There are many facts connected with the Eternal Verities which you cannot deny, but you do not know enough of God in your own souls to give you the personal assurance of their truth. The result is a sense of restlessness, dissatisfaction and incompleteness. . . .

It is possible—nay, indeed, it is probable—that the preaching of the cross of our Lord Jesus Christ is your great stumbling-block. Concerning the atonement, is it not true that you " see too much for denial and too little for assurance " ?

Yet it is at this cross that the saints have learnt the unfathomable love of God, and the secret of holy living. " God forbid," said the apostle, " that I should glory, save in the cross of our Lord Jesus Christ, by whom the world is crucified unto me and I unto the world." A writer of two centuries ago has said : " Christ crucified is the library which triumphant souls will be studying in to all eternity."*

The Lord hath need of you. The Church, with its call to new activities, is waiting for your emancipation.

We beseech you to recognise the urgency of the spiritual situation ; *your* contracted and hesitating life ; and *our* great need for your Christian service and testimony. It cannot be the will of your heavenly Father that your life should be unfruitful. Where you have found footholds for your faith, press forward. . . . Make the throne of grace your continual resort. Instead of scattering the seeds of doubt, take all your difficulties to your Father in heaven, and reason with Him about them, and then, in the silence of your whole being, wait for His conclusions concerning your attitude of mind and heart.

We press upon you the importance of a renewed and increased study of the Holy Scriptures. They are still able to make wise unto salvation through faith which is in Christ Jesus. Even if there be questions still unresolved, you will at least admit, with Coleridge, as you carefully and reverently ponder the sacred writings, that the Scriptures find you as nothing else does. From them you will learn that the language of the Christian is not one of doubt, but of assurance. The inspired writers knew Him whom they believed, and were persuaded that He was able to keep that which they had committed unto Him. Their assurance was from the earnest of the Spirit in their hearts.

If your doubts seem to gather around the person of our

* Stillingfleet's *Origines Sacrae*, 1663 edition, p. 605.

Lord Jesus Christ, we lovingly advise you to search these same Scriptures, and you will find that they testify of Him. The first chapter of the Gospel of John and the first chapters of the Epistles to the Colossians and to the Hebrews are amongst the most precious of those words of God which bear witness concerning His Son. " It pleased the Father that in Him should all fullness dwell."

If the Cross of Christ is either an offence or a stumbling-block to you, we entreat you to study prayerfully those chapters in the Gospels which speak of the dying of our Lord. Listen in silence to His last words as they penetrate the abyss of human need ; until with head bent and heart made tender, you, too, may say : " Truly this was the Son of God."—From the *Yearly Meeting Epistle*, 1903.

Science and Religion

The scientific we shall find inadequate, because by itself the study of nature cannot lead us to the knowledge of a God who answers the questions of the heart and satisfies its craving. Nature shows us law in every nook and cranny of the Universe, but it cannot reveal a God of personal love. Some people think it can, but the real truth is that, like the Roman Catholic in his cult of the Virgin, they read into the goddess or principle they call Nature that which they have unconsciously borrowed from Jesus Christ. To be strictly scientific in the accepted sense of the term, is to be strictly agnostic. Science has its legitimate field and its legitimate methods, although, like the theologian at whom he so often girds, the scientist is not without his prejudices and his narrow dogmatism. He is to be respected when he speaks according to what he knows. His knowledge is at least something more learned by man about God. Unless we are to fall into an ancient fallacy and exclude God from His universe, we must regard every fact of science as a fresh revelation of His creative activity and power. Nevertheless, scientific knowledge lies on a plane different from that on which the knowledge we seek is to be found. . . . [It] cannot help a man to resist a present temptation or to face death with Christian confidence and hope. Science by itself is, and must always remain, powerless to give us a God who will draw out the tendrils of the human heart towards Himself.—John Wilhelm Rowntree, *Essays and Addresses*, 1906, pp. 387, 388.

The modern method of enquiry by experiment and inference, by inductive generalisation and subsequent verification, has been amazingly fruitful in the better understanding of physical nature. But the very precision of its intellectual processes, and the inevitableness of the garnered results are sometimes urged against it, as tending to cramp and warp the perception of other kinds of truth. It is charged sometimes with leading men to reject or despise other kinds of truth which have not been discovered by the same sort of process, and which cannot be verified by experiment, weighed in the balance, or analysed in the test-tube. Doubtless there is some ground for this reflection. In any department of human activity the too-exclusive exercise of any one faculty or set of faculties tends to bring about a one-sided development ; and the neglect of any faculty tends to its atrophy. Perhaps the worst that can be said against devotion to the discovery of truth in the physical sciences is that it tends to impose a necessitarian or determinist view of existence. When we find in physics that through all there runs an inescapable relation of cause and effect ; that nothing happens except that which follows from antecedent causes ; we are apt to conclude— though quite erroneously—that the whole world is ruled by fate, by fixed and determinate necessity, affording no scope for free-will or for the operation of moral forces. Such a view would reduce the universe to a mere mechanism and remove all moral responsibility from man ; a view to be sternly repelled. —Swarthmore Lecture, 1915, Silvanus Phillips Thompson, *The Quest for Truth*, pp. 47, 48.

Unity in Diversity

"There are as many unveilings of God as there are saintly souls,"* and day after day the central thought of Unity in

     * John the Scot, *De Divisione Naturae*, 1669.

Diversity, the true unity, has been present with us and has unfolded itself more clearly. We have realised that in our own Society, and among many of our Christian brethren beyond its borders, there are at the same time wide differences of method and a oneness of aim. Especially when it is difficult to appreciate each other's point of view, we try to remember that to faithful seekers, though the roads may be many, yet the goal is one.

We are not scattered or alone. A vision comes to us of the Captain of our Salvation.

" And it came to pass, when Joshua was by Jericho, that he lifted up his eyes and looked, and, behold, there stood a man over against him with his sword drawn in his hand ; and Joshua went unto him, and said unto him, Art thou for us or for our adversaries ? And he said, Nay ; but as captain of the host of the Lord am I now come."

The well-known verses, the story, familiar to us from our childhood, may perhaps be allowed to take on a new meaning as we catch a glimpse of what the true unity must be.

Art thou for us, or for our adversaries ; or—and this is perhaps harder still—art thou for those with whom we do not see eye to eye ; art thou indeed for them ? And above all the clamour of our discordant voices, our jarring opinions, comes the age-long unchanging answer : Neither for this wing nor for that ; nay, but as leader of the whole army—as captain of the Lord's host am I come.

With Christ as leader and commander, who shall be afraid ? The weakest among us will be nerved to new courage by His victorious presence in our midst. The strongest as they hear His call will give themselves to loyal service. Under His controlling will all His host shall march forward with unity of purpose against the world-wide forces of sin.

Accepting His leadership, there is revealed to us in the fullness of time a tenderer figure—our risen Lord and Master standing, not, as of old, by the seashore of Galilee, but radiant in the dawn light of a new day, beside the ocean of eternal love.

Ever as the tide rises to fill and overflow and join together all the separate pools along the shore, we hear His voice calling still to every human soul, "Follow Me." "Follow Me"—to daily duties, to the great adventure, even to the Cross, it is all one obedience. "Follow Me," the one call sounded at the beginning and at the end of His ministry on earth, and ringing on through all the centuries. We read of those earliest disciples that they arose and left their nets, those nets their hope of livelihood, left them with their slippery entangling meshes still unmended, and followed Him. Of course they followed Him ; what else can even His feeblest disciples do but follow if they once "know His voice"?

And this "Divine Love imposeth no rigorous or unreasonable commands, but graciously points out the spirit of brotherhood and the way to happiness."* . . .

We can safely leave our troubled issues in His hands, and yet bear, with Him, the burden and the joy of their slow working out. In those hands the many threads are woven into one perfect whole.

Through Him we enter into that unity of redeemed souls everywhere, which is no intellectual achievement, but rather the climate and atmosphere of daily life. Not in our notions about Him but in the power of His healing presence among us, do we become aware of the one Christ. In His own Person we perceive, even with our dim and clouded vision, the same mysterious unity in diversity. He who is the complete Christ, divine and human, is, as we have been reverently reminded, the Christ both of history and of inward experience.†

He calls us to follow Him fully in the path of Love. When we think of the conditions of the world, a sense of dismay and helplessness threatens to overwhelm us. To oppose hatred and anger and selfishness only with meekness and gentleness—is not this to court defeat? Doubtless it would be so, were it not true that God is love, and that therefore those who live

---

* *ante*, p. 121.
† Edward Grubb, *Swarthmore Lecture*, 1914—"The Historic and the Inward Christ."

in the spirit of love have on their side the creative Power which has made and which sustains the universe. Our Father made the world in which we live, and love cannot be finally overthrown. Apparent failure we need not fear. Our Saviour laid down His life for us in fulfilling perfectly the law of love. As we take to ourselves the full meaning of His Cross, we find that we too are called to follow in the way of love, even if it lead us to shame and defeat, in the great assurance that we shall be led, together with all faithful souls, to share in the triumph of the Lord of Love.—From the *Yearly Meeting Epistle*, 1914.

Unity in the Spirit

Are we going to seek for unity only in those points about which we are all agreed ? or shall we try to find it also in those things wherein we differ ? Hitherto the first method has been tried, and tried throughout the centuries in vain. Are we not coming to see that it is our points of difference also that will make our future union possible ? It is as if, all this time, Christendom had been striving to build for itself a body out of a heap of scattered bones, and had thought that the only way to do it was to try by cutting and sawing to make all the bones exactly the same shape and size. Whereas the world is now beginning to see that if only the Spirit of Life were blowing with sufficient strength to make those bones live, then every point of difference whether great or small would reveal itself as no mistake, but rather as the divinely ordered adjustment to the function in the living body that each particular bone was intended to perform. . . . The unity of Christians is not in our judgment something that needs to be artificially created ; it is already here, and only needs to be recognised and acted on. We have unity with " all those who love our Lord Jesus Christ in uncorruptness," and in whose lives His character is being manifested, whatever diversities there may be in the formulas by which they express themselves, or in the practices by which they seek to cherish His life on their souls.—From paper on *The True Basis of Christian Unity*, presented to the *Yearly Meeting*,

1917, by its Commission appointed in connection with the *World Conference on Faith and Order*.

He that keeps not a day may unite in the same Spirit, in the same life, in the same love, with him that keeps a day; and he who keeps a day may unite in heart and soul with the same Spirit and life in him who keeps not a day; but he that judgeth the other because of either of these errs from the Spirit, from the love, from the life, and so breaks the bond of unity. . . . And here is the true unity, in the Spirit, in the inward life, and not in an outward uniformity. . . . Men keeping close to God, the Lord will lead them on fast enough . . . for He taketh care of such, and knoweth what light and what practices are most proper for them. . . . And oh, how sweet and pleasant is it to the truly spiritual eye to see several sorts of believers, several forms of Christians in the school of Christ, every one learning their own lesson, performing their own peculiar service, and knowing, owning, and loving one another in their several places and different performances to their Master. . . . The great error of the ages of the apostasy hath been to set up an outward order and uniformity and to make men's consciences bend thereto, either by arguments of wisdom, or by force; but the property of the true Church government is to leave the conscience to its full liberty in the Lord, to preserve it single and entire for the Lord to exercise, and to seek unity in the Light and in the Spirit, walking sweetly and harmoniously together in the midst of different practices.—Isaac Penington, *Works*, 1681 edition, Part I, pp. 240, 241.

Thou, O Christ, convince us by Thy Spirit; thrill us with Thy divine passion; drown our selfishness in Thy invading Love; lay on us the burden of the world's suffering; drive us forth with the apostolic fervour of the early Church! So only can our message be delivered. "Speak to the Children of Israel that they go forward." —John Wilhelm Rowntree, *Essays and Addresses* p. xlvii.

Remember then, O my soul, the quietude of those in whom Christ governs, and in all thy proceedings feel after it.

Doth He condescend to bless thee with His presence? To move and influence thee to action? To dwell and to walk in thee? Remember then thy station as being sacred to God. Accept of the strength freely offered to thee, and take heed that no weakness in conforming to unwise, expensive and hard-hearted customs, gendering to discord and strife, be given way to. Doth He claim my body as His temple, and graciously require that I may be sacred to Him? Oh, that I may prize this favour, and that my whole life may be conformable to this character! Remember, O my soul, that the Prince of Peace is thy Lord; that He communicates His unmixed wisdom to His family, that they, living in perfect simplicity, may give no just cause of offence to any creature, but that they may walk as He walked.—John Woolman, *Journal*, New Century edition, p. 191.

INDEX OF PERSONS AND AUTHORITIES

All Friends' Conference, 1920, Minute and Message on Peace Testimony, 124

" Apology ", Barclay's, 29-31, 73, 98-9, 103

Appeal to All Men, 1919, 81

Askew, Mary, 13

Audland, John, 31

Augustine, Saint, 68

Bacon, Sir Francis, 45

Baker, Daniel, 25

Balby Meeting of Elders, 1656, viii

Barclay, Robert, 29-31, 73, 98-9, 103

Besse, " Sufferings ", 24-6

Barbados, Epistle to the Governor of, vi, 66-8, 98

Bible, Quotations from the Old Testament—
> Genesis v. 24, 126 ; xxii. 18, 89
> Joshua v. 13-14, 135
> Psalms xlii. 3, 82 ; li. 10, 57 ; li. 16-17, 106
> Isaiah ix. 6-7, 89 ; liii. 4-6, 89 ; lx. 20, 131
> Jeremiah i. 5, 23 ; xxiii. 6, 89 ; xxxi. 31, 116

Bible, Quotations from the New Testament—
> Matthew v. 34, 116 ; v. 44, 116 ; vii. 7, 63 ; x. 8, 107 ; x. 25, 121 ; xi. 28, 57, 94 ; xvi. 24, 110 ; xviii. 3, 105 ; xxvi. 28, 116 ; xxvi. 39, 7 ; xxvii. 46, 7 ; xxvii. 54, 133
> Mark i. 16-20, 136 ; vi. 5, 109 ; viii. 36, 80 ; x. 14, 118
> John i. 1-4, 90 ; i. 14, 101 ; i. 29, 67 ; iii. 4, 105 ; iii. 7, 105 ; iv. 14, 90 ; iv. 24, 115 ; v. 39, 102 ; vi. 35, 90 ; vi. 63, 117 ; x. 1-3, 39 ; x. 4, 136 ; x. 27, 90 ; x. 35, 100 ;

xiv. 6, 69 ; xiv. 9, 84 ; xiv. 15, 1 ; xiv. 16, 117 ; xv. 9, 117 ; xvii. 11, 117 ; xvii. 22, 3 ; xx. 31, 100 ; xxi. 19, 135

Acts iii. 22, 23, 67

Romans ii. 28, 13, 113 ; iii. 23, 92 ; v. 8, 92 ; viii. 2, 116 ; xii. 1, 107 ; xv. 4, 100

1 Corinthians i. 23, 95 ; x. 31, 107, 109 ; xi. 26, 115 ; xii. 11, 106 ; xiii. 7, 82

2 Corinthians iii. 6, 113 ; iii. 18, 75 ; v. 14, 15, 1

Galatians ii. 20, 40, 87, 126 ; vi. 2, 81 ; vi. 14, 132

Ephesians ii. 3, 75 ; ii. 18, 115 ; vi. 24, 137

Philippians iii. 10, 95

Colossians i. 14, 89 ; i. 15-17, 90 ; i. 19, 133 ; ii. 9, 90.

1 Timothy ii. 5, 115 ; vi. 16, 108

2 Timothy i. 12, 132 ; iii. 15, 132 ; iii. 15-16, 100

Hebrews i. 3, 90 ; ii. 16, 89 ; iii. 1, 91 ; iv. 15, 91, 92 ; vii. 25, 90 ; viii. 8, 9, 116 ; xii. 24, 90 ; xii. 27, 131

1 Peter ii. 5, 107 ; ii. 24, 47

2 Peter i. 21, 99, 100

1 John ii. 2, 75, 89, 105 ; v. 20, 67

Jude 3, 47

Revelation iii. 20, 109, 115, 117 ; v. 13, 91 ; xxii. 17, 75

Boston Martyrs, The, 21-5

Bowden, " History of Friends in America ", 18-21

Bownas, Samuel, 38-9

Braithwaite, Joseph Bevan, 52-4

Bright, John, 47-9

Bristol and Frenchay Monthly Meeting, Testimony to Robert Charleton, 46-7

Burrough, Edward, 17, 18, 73, 104

Cairns, David S., 83
Camm, John, 31
Caton, William, 12, 13
Charleton, Robert, 46
Chevers, Sarah, 25
Christison, Wenlock, 22
Clayton, Anne, 12, 13
Coleridge, S. T., quoted in Yorkshire Q.M. Statement, 1919, and Yearly Meeting Epistle, 1903, 102, 132
Corder, S., " Life of Elizabeth Fry ", 44
Cotton, Priscilla, 26
Crosfield, George, " Memoirs of S. Fothergill ", 41

Dent, William, 52
Dewsbury, William, 9-12, 71-2
Doudney, Richard, 21
Dyer, Mary, 24

Ellwood, Thomas, 8, 33-5
Endicott, Governor, 22
Evans, Katharine, 25-6

Faith and Order, Commission on, 2-4, 64-5, 76-8, 137
Farnsworth, Richard, 12, 14
Fell, Margaret (afterwards Fox), 12-14
Fothergill, Samuel, 41-2
Fowler, Robert, 18-21
Fox, George, vi, 2, 5-8, 12-14, 17, 19, 66-8, 69, 71, 75, 87, 88, 98, 114-115, 123
" Friends and Fellow Seekers ", 124
Fry, Elizabeth, 43-5

Gibbons, Sarah, 21
Gillett, George, 51
Glover, T. R., 83
Grellet, Stephen, 45-6, 114
Grubb, Edward, 136
Grubb, Sarah (Lynes), 42-3

Hare, A. J. C., " The Gurneys of Earlham ", 43-5
Hodgkin, Thomas, 44, 60-2, 113-14
Hodgson, Robert, 21
Howgill, Francis, 17-18, 72

Inquisition at Malta, 25

John the Scot, " De Divisione Naturae ", 1669, 134
Jordans Conference of Young Friends, 1920, 125-6

Law, William (quoted by J. W. Rowntree), 55
Leddra, William, 22
London and Middlesex Quarterly Meeting Statement on the Scriptures, 1918, 101

Meeting for Sufferings' " Appeal to all Men ", 1919, 81
Message " To Friends and Fellow Seekers ", 124
Morley, Lord, on John Bright, 48

Nayler, James, 2, 14, 15-17
Norton, Humphrey, 20

Pascal (quoted in Y.M. Epistle, 1903), 131
Pearson, Anthony, 15
Penington, Isaac, viii, 9, 26-9, 33, 100, 108, 138
Penn, William, viii, 8-9, 32-3, 35, 62-3, 109-12

Rich, Robert (words of James Nayler), 16-17
Roberts, Gerrard, 19
Robinson, William, 22, 24
Rowntree, John Stephenson, 109, 114
Rowntree, John Wilhelm, 2, 54-8, 93-4, 118, 133, 139
Rowntree, Joshua, 52

Salthouse, Thomas, 12, 13
Savery, William, 43, 44
Seebohm, Benjamin, " Memoirs of S. Grellet ", 45-6
Seekers, The Westmorland, 17-18
Skipton General Meeting, 1660, Epistle from, 122-3

Springett, Gulielma Maria (afterwards Penn), 33
Stephen, Caroline E., 58-9, 108
Stevens, Priest, and George Fox, 7
Stevenson, Marmaduke, 21-4
Stillingfleet, "Origines Sacrae", 1663, 132
Stirredge, Elizabeth, 31
Story, Thomas, 35-7
Swarthmore Household, Account of, 15
Swarthmore Lectures :
    1911. T. Hodgkin, 44
    1912. T. R. Glover, 83
    1913. J. Rowntree, 52
    1914. E. Grubb, 136
    1915. S. P. Thompson, 134

Tennyson, Alfred, Lord, "In Memoriam", 70
Thomas, Richard H., 100-1, 113
Thompson, Silvanus P., 112-13, 134
Thornton, Samuel, 33-4
"True Basis of Christian Unity", 2-4, 137

Waterhouse, Elizabeth (quoting I. Penington), viii
Watson, Robert Spence, 108
Waugh, Dorothy, 21
Weatherhead, Mary, 21
Westmorland Seekers, The, 17-18
Whittier, John Greenleaf, 49-51
    Back to thyself is measured well, 128
    Believe and trust. Through stars and suns, 130
    Dear Lord and Father of Mankind, 129
    Early hath Life's mighty question, 127
    I bow my forehead to the dust, 50
    In calm and cool and silence, once again, 50
    In joy of inward peace, or sense, 96
    No fable old, nor mythic lore, 94
Wilson, Anne, 38

Woodhead, Lucy Anne, 59-60
"Woodhouse", Voyage of the, 18-21
Woolman, John, 39-40, 120-2, 124, 139

Yearly Meeting, Adjourned, 1916, Minute re Peace, 123
Yearly Meeting of Ministers, 1676, Epistle, 103
Yearly Meeting, 1829, Minute re Division in U.S.A., 89-91
Yearly Meeting, 1841, Address on Authority of Christ, 106
Yearly Meeting, 1920, A Word to All who seek Truth, 78-81
Yearly Meeting Epistles :
    1736. The Work of Jesus Christ, 88
    1827. Creeds, 64
    1830. The Operations of the Spirit, 74
    1835. Spiritual Worship and Outward Rites, 115
    1836. The Scriptures, 100
    1852. The Work of Jesus Christ, 91
    1854. Membership, 105
    1857. An Effectual Witness, 73
    1861. The Operations of the Spirit 74
    1866. Worship of God, 105
    1868. The Operations of the Spirit, 74
    1868. The Offering up of Christ, 93
    1868. The Work of Jesus Christ, 92
    1879. He Died for All, 75
    1880. Spiritual Worship and Outward Rites, 115-17
    1881. The Work of Jesus Christ, 92
    1881. Membership, 105
    1889. Walking with God, 126
    1894. Service in Daily Life, 119
    1895. Jesus and the Children, 95
    1899. Spiritual Priesthood, 107
    1903. Religious Difficulties, 131

Yearly Meeting Epistles (*continued*):
1904. Preaching Jesus, 95
1905. Reality in Religion, 1-2
1906. Christ Within and the Christ of History, 87
1907. The Message of the Society of Friends, 68
1909. The Cross of Christ, 94
1911. Service in Daily Life, 118
1912. The Nature of God, 82
1914. Unity in Diversity, 134
1915. The Nature of God, 82
1920. Seeing God in the Face of Jesus Christ, 83-5
Yorkshire Quarterly Meeting, 1919, Statement of, 86, 101
Young Friends' International Conference, 1920, Minute of, 125-6

INDEX OF SUBJECTS

Adventure, The Spirit of, 80, 85

Aim of the Book, vi-viii

Animals, Kindness to, 122

Appeal to All Men, 81

Asceticism, 56, 110

Assurance, Spiritual, 11, 12, 16, 25, 29, 46, 51, 54

Atonement, The (*see also* " Christ, the Saviour "), 46, 54, 88-95

Authority of Christ in His Church, 106

Authority, Revolt against, 77

Baptism, 77, 113, 117, 118, 120

Baptism of the Holy Spirit, 77, 113, 117, 118, 120

Belief, Faith, and, 2

Best in Every Man, Appeal to the, 126

Bible, a Library, 100

Bible, Inspiration of the, 64, 66, 71, 89, 98, 102

Bible, Use of the, 39, 49, 54, 132

Birth, The Second, 28, 69, 72, 94, 105

Brotherhood, The Spirit of, 124

Business as a Way of Service, 118

Business Meetings, Conduct of, 104

Calvinism, 18, 30

Canon of Scripture, 101

Children, 95, 105, 118

Christ, All in all to the Believer, 29, 55, 87, 88, 96

Christ, Authority of, in His Church, 106

Christ, Commands of, 116

Christ, Cross of, 93

Christ, The Head of His Church, 3, 26, 90, 135-6

Christ, Human and Divine, 86

Christ, The Judge, 90

Christ, The Leader, 32, 135

Christ, The Life, 87

Christ, The Light of, in the Heart, 6, 7, 8, 13, 17, 28, 29, 31, 34, 39, 63, 71-81, 86, 109

Christ, The Love of, 1, 61, 95, 136

Christ, Nigh to All, 73

Christ, The Offering up of, 93

Christ, The Personality of, 29, 64, 66, 86-97, 132

Christ, The Place of, 88

Christ, The Revealer of God, 3, 6, 61, 68, 83, 84, 93, 94, 101, 123, 124

Christ, The Saviour, 1, 6, 7, 10, 11, 32, 36, 41, 46, 47, 52, 53, 54-6, 64, 66, 68, 71, 74, 75, 80, 86, 88, 93, 109, 131-3

Christ, Union with, 1, 3, 11, 28, 36, 41, 57, 63, 87, 94, 118, 126, 135

Christ Within and Christ of History, 86

Christ, The Work of, 88

Christianity, True, viii, 2, 3, 53, 59-60, 62, 103, 110, 118-19

Church, The Building of the, 112

Church, The Call to serve by the, 1, 132

Church, The Nature of the, 103-7

Competition in Business, 118

Conscience distinguished from the " Inner Light ", 74

Conscience and Christ, 56

Conscience, Freedom of, 138

Consideration for Others, 120, 121

Consistency in Principle and Life, 77

Conversion, Experience of:
    Samuel Bownas, 38-9
    Joseph Bevan Braithwaite, 52
    Robert Charleton, 46
    William Dewsbury, 11
    Samuel Fothergill, 41
    Early Friends, 8
    Elizabeth Fry, 44
    George Gillett, 51
    Stephen Grellet, 45

Conversion, Necessity of, 105

Convincements, *see* Spiritual Experiences of Friends, 5-63

Creation, The, 66, 120, 133

Creed, Limitations of a, 4

Creed, Position of Friends as to, 64

Cross, The Meaning of the, 1, 7, 26, 32, 69, 87, 93, 94, 95, 111, 124, 131-2, 137

Death, Lines on, 60

Declaring Truth in Streets and Markets, 42

Dedication of Heart, 18, 35-6, 63, 69, 107, 114, 138

Distribution of Wealth, Unequal, 120

Doctrinal Statements, 64, 65, 66-70

Doctrines, Place of, 2, 3

Domination *versus* Co-operation, 124-5

Doubt, 131

Dying, The Fear of, 60-1

England a " Family of Prophets ", 122

Experience, A Christianity of, 3, 4

Faith and Belief, 2

Faith of a Quaker, 2, 118

Faith, The Work of, 109

Family Worship, 48, 49, 98

Fear as a Spiritual Experience, 10, 31

Fellowship, The Experience of and Need for real, 2, 16, 18, 70, 80, 84, 112, 124, 125

Following Christ, 44, 112, 124, 135

Forgiving Spirit, 16, 56

Formalism, Dangers of, 3, 4, 8, 39, 54, 62, 104

Foundations of a True Social Order, 124

Friends, Experiences of Early, Recorded by W. Penn, 8-9

God, His Fatherhood, 28, 60, 73, 81, 93-4, 125-6, 129, 130

God, His Nature and Goodness, 50, 51, 58, 66, 79, 84, 92, 94, 111, 123, 124, 130

God, His Real Presence, 18, 23, 28, 36, 46, 68-9, 114, 115, 118, 119

God, Imperfect Ideas of, 15, 83

God, Knowing, 28, 63, 73, 130, 133

God of Things as they are meant to be (*See also* " Christ " and " Love "), 124

God, The Creator, 66, 90, 111, 120, 133

God, The Free Grace of, 71

God, The Love of, 6, 17, 23, 25, 35, 51, 52, 61, 69, 82, 137

God, The Peace of, 37, 129

God, The Power of, 10, 14, 17, 31, 43, 82, 93, 103, 136

God, The Revelation of, in Jesus Christ, 3, 61, 69-70, 84-5, 93-4, 124

God, The Universality of His Grace, 8, 51, 60, 71, 75, 76, 79, 82-85, 108, 123

God, The Will of, 3, 24, 25, 32, 50, 109, 110, 113

God, The Worship of, 105

Gospel, Fulfilment of God's Promises in the, 92, 116

Growth, Spiritual, 56, 73

Guidance, Divine, viii, 18-21, 22-4, 49, 77, 79, 119

Heart, A Tender, 122

Heart, Dedication of, *see* " Dedication of Heart "

He Died for All, 75

Hunger, Spiritual, 11, 27-8, 31

Identification with the World's Sin and Misery, 39-40

Incarnation, Thoughts on the, 86

Inconsistency of Christians, 39, 62, 119

Individualism and its Limitation, 79

Industrial Reconstruction, 85, 124

Inspiration of the Bible, 64, 66, 71, 89, 98-102

Inspiration as it came to Thomas Story, 35

Inward Law, The, 46, 47

Jesus and the Children, 95

Kingdom of God, The Law of the, 1

Kingdom of God, A Present Experience, 17-18

Kingdom of Heaven on Earth, 125

Law, Human and Divine, 109

Life as more Important than Theory, 30, 77, 90, 108

Life, a Sacrament, 70, 107, 114

Life, Religion a Way of, 108-30

Life, Power of a Quiet, 52

Light of Christ Within, 63, 71, 74, 81, 108

Light of the Holy Spirit (*see also* " Spirit, The Indwelling "), 76

Little Things, Importance of, 31

Love, a Constraining Power, 1, 81, 82, 136

Love of God, its Fullness, 25, 69, 82, 91

Love of God, its Saving Power, 47, 57, 73, 91, 109

Love, Life to be lived in, 80, 121-2, 136

Love, A Measure of the same, 72

Maintenance of Christian Workers, 106
Marriage as a Sacrament, 114
Materialism, Danger of, 83
Meeting, Devotion to a Friends', 60
Meeting, Effect of a Friends', 27, 30, 33, 36, 38, 45, 51, 58
Membership, Church, 105
Message of the Society of Friends, 68
Ministers, Testimonies to Deceased, 46, 49, 52
Ministry, Experience of the :
  John Audland, 31
  Samuel Bownas, 38
  Robert Charleton, 46
  Thomas Ellwood, 33
  George Fox, 7
  Early Friends, 8
  Elizabeth Fry, 43
  Sarah (Lynes) Grubb, 42
Ministry not Confined to one Class, 105, 106
Ministry, The Call to the, 42, 46, 76, 105, 106
Missionary Service, The Call to, 122, 123
Moral Law Applicable to States, 48

Negative Christianity, 54
Notional Religion, 7

Oaths, 116
Obedience to the Divine Presence, 70
Ocean of Darkness and Death, 6
One-sided Development, 134
Opportunity, Equality of, 125
Order, The New World, 85, 124
Organisation, Limits to, 76
Our Lord and Master, 96
Ownership of Material Things, 125

Peace, Testimony for, 123
Perception of the Light of God, 78
Persecution of Quakers, 15, 21-6, 116
Personality, Importance of, 125, 126
Personality, Influence of, 70
Personality of Christ, 64, 66, 82-97, 132
Philanthropic Work of Friends, 47, 48
Political Life, Friends and, 48, 49
Popularity, Danger of, 44
Positive Truth rather than Negative, 118

Possessions, The Snare of, 85, 120-1, 125
Prayer, Examples of :
  George Fox, 7-8
  Isaac Penington, 28
  John Wilhelm Rowntree, 57
Prayer, The Need for, 127, 132
Preaching Jesus, 95
Pre-arrangement in Religious Exercise, 106
Presence in the Midst, 17, 20, 28, 37, 58, 113, 119
Priesthood, Spiritual, 107
Priests, Called to be, 76, 107, 115
Prisons like Palaces, 2, 9, 11
Problems, Religious, 131-8
Progress, The Meaning of, 80
Progressive Character of Revelation, 3-4, 101
Protection, Divine, 19-20, 31
Proxy, Worship impossible by, 113, 116

Quakerism, The Meaning of, 1-4, 118, 126
Quakers Persecuted, 15, 21-6, 116

Reality in Religion, 1, 78
Recluse Life, Argument against a, 110, 113
Religion a Way of Life, 108
Religious Problems, 131
Return Home to Within, 72
Revisions of the Book of Discipline, vi
Right, The Pursuit of, 48, 119
Ritual, Views upon, 77, 113-18
Rome, Church of, 30, 45

Sacrament, Life a, 43, 70, 107, 114
Sacraments, Friends' Attitude to the (see also " Ritual, Views upon " and " Supper, The Lord's "), 77
Sacrifice Required of All, 70, 111, 124
Salvation, 11, 41, 42, 46, 51, 54-8
Science and Religion, 133
Scriptures Expounded by G. Fox, 7, 13, 71
Scriptures, The, 89, 132
Scriptures, Witness to Christ in the, 15, 99
Secular and Religious, 48, 70, 106, 109
Seed, The, 8, 11, 28, 63, 67, 68, 73, 81, 122, 124

Seekers in Westmorland, The, 12, 17
Selfishness, The Sin of, 55, 87
Service Abroad, 122
Service in Daily Life, 118, 126
Service, the Purpose of Salvation, 1, 70
Shining Through All, 71
Silence, The Place of, 17, 30, 37, 50, 58-9, 112
Simplicity of Life, 2, 119, 120-1, 125
Sin, Consciousness of :
    William Dewsbury, 10-11
    Thomas Ellwood, 34
    Margaret Fell, 14
    Samuel Fothergill, 41
    George Gillett, 51
    Stephen Grellet, 45
    Sarah (Lynes) Grubb, 42
    Isaac Penington, 27
    Elizabeth Stirredge, 31
    John Greenleaf Whittier, 50
Sin, Forgiveness of, 66, 89, 93
Sin in the Sight of God, 93
Sin, The Fact of, 64, 71, 92, 93
Sincerity in Life and Word, 48, 55
Singing, 10
Slavery, Economic, 120
Slavery, Efforts to abolish, 39, 49, 77
Social Order, The, 118-19, 124-5
Society, The Redemption of, 1
Spirit that Delights to do no Evil, 16
Spirit, The Indwelling, 5, 7-10, 21, 28-9, 34, 48, 63, 64, 68-81, 87, 88, 95, 109-11, 117, 126
Spirit, Leadership of the, 76
Spirit, Operations of the, 74
Spirit, Witness to the Scriptures of the, 13, 99
Spirit, Work of the Holy, 76, 117
Spiritual Experiences of Friends, 5-63
Spiritual Worship and Outward Rites, 113
Sufferings, Joy amid, 2, 6, 11, 17, 21, 25-6
Supper, The Lord's, 10, 77, 114, 115, 116, 117, 118
Swarthmore Hall, 12-15
Symbols, unnecessary, 64, 77, 113, 115

Traditional Quakerism and Christianity (see " Formalism, Dangers of ")

True Social Order, Foundations of a, 124
Truth a Possession, 62
Truth, George Fox's Labour for, 7, 8
Truth a Shadow and a Substance, viii
Truth, Progressively apprehended, 4, 65
Truth, Ultimate, to be sought, 3-4, 78, 126, 134

Unity and Concord, 104
Unity of Life, Sacred and Secular, 63, 69, 107, 108-9
Unity in Diversity, 79, 134-8
Unity, True Basis of, 3, 18, 79, 81, 113, 117, 135-8
Unity with God, 76, 84, 126
Unity of all Religious Souls, 111
Universality of the Possibility of Christian Experience, 3, 76

Victory through Christ, 32, 57, 95, 123, 135
Virgin Birth, 66

Walking with God, 126
War, Opposition to, 10, 48, 49, 123, 124
Way of Life, The, 34, 84, 108-30
Wealth, Unequal Distribution of, 120
Westmorland Seekers, 12, 17
Will, Surrender of the :
    William Dewsbury, 10
    Mary Dyer, 24
    Robert Fowler, 18
    Early Friends, 8
    Sarah (Lynes) Grubb, 42
    Thomas Story, 35
    John Greenleaf Whittier, 49
    John Woolman, 39
    Yearly Meeting Epistle, 1907, 70
Witness, An Effectual, 73
Women, Equality of, with Men, 76, 107
Word, The, and the Words of God, 98, 101, 108
Word to All who seek Truth, 78-80
Worship in the Life of the Church, 103
Worship of God, 105
Worship, True, 36, 50, 77, 78, 105, 113, 115, 120

Yearly Meeting, Effect of, on J. B. Braithwaite, 53